UNINTENDED
IMPACT

ONE ATHLETE'S JOURNEY FROM CONCUSSIONS
IN AMATEUR FOOTBALL TO CTE DEMENTIA

[signature]

80 ~ 1965

UNINTENDED IMPACT

ONE ATHLETE'S JOURNEY FROM CONCUSSIONS IN AMATEUR FOOTBALL TO CTE DEMENTIA

JIM PROEBSTLE

FOREWORD BY ROBERT A. STERN, PhD

BOSTON UNIVERSITY SCHOOL OF MEDICINE

BEAVER'S
POND
PRESS

Unintended Impact is a creative nonfiction memoir. As such, it is based on my memories as to events and how they occurred. I recognize that characters described in this book may have memories of the events described that are different than my own. Extensive editorial precautions have been taken to ensure diligence to the factual accuracy of Dick's life.

The views and opinions expressed in this book are those of the authors and do not reflect the position of the publisher.

Edited by Angela Weichmann

ISBN 13: 978-1-59298-883-9

Library of Congress Catalog Number: 2015904254

Printed in the United States of America
First Printing: 2015

19   18   17   16   15   5   4   3   2   1

Cover and interior design by James Monroe Design, LLC.

Beaver's Pond Press, Inc.
7108 Ohms Lane
Edina, MN 55439–2129
BEAVER'S POND PRESS   (952) 829-8818
www.BeaversPondPress.com

An offensive lineman's first job is to protect his quarterback.
Dick was my quarterback.

CONTENTS

SECTION III
CTE OUTCOME—YOUR BRAIN LOSES CONTROL

SECTION IV
CTE CLOSING MOMENTS—YOUR BRAIN IS
BEYOND REPAIR

FOREWORD

In October 2012, I had the honor of conducting an extensive telephone interview with the family members of Dick Proebstle, one of the "Legend Donors" to our Brain Bank at the Boston University Center for the Study of Traumatic Encephalopathy. While my colleague Dr. Ann McKee and her team conduct the neuropathological examinations of the brain tissue of the deceased donors, my role is to find out as much as I can about the brain donors' lives, including medical history, brain trauma, and sports history, and details about the type and course of any changes in cognition, mood, behavior, and movement.

During that phone call in autumn 2012, I learned about a wonderful man—a husband, father, and brother. A man who once was a talented amateur athlete and competitive business opportunist. A man who died at age sixty-nine with a diagnosis of "dementia" after years of struggling with memory impairments, disorganization, poor problem solving, significant personality and behavioral changes, and problems with movement. I began to learn about the "man" and not merely the "brain donor"—an individual with a loving family who suffered through the changes and decline of their loved one.

Approximately two months later, I had another phone call with the family, but this time, my colleague and world-renowned neuropathologist, Dr. McKee, joined us to provide the results of her examination. The results demonstrated what I had predicted from hearing of Mr. Proebstle's history: he had the telltale signs of Chronic Traumatic Encephalopathy, or CTE. His brain had been slowly destroyed by a widespread deposition of an abnormal form of a protein called tau. The loss of brain tissue and the destruction of neurons had led to Mr. Proebstle's decline and, ultimately, his death. Hearing the diagnosis of CTE provided some form of answer to the question of what caused the long, confusing, and dramatic decline of this husband, father, and brother. As it had done with so many of our cases before (and as it has done countless times since), the diagnosis of CTE provided perhaps more than an answer; it provided some closure or resolution.

The author, Jim Proebstle, presents a sensitive, moving, and gripping account of his brother Dick's downward spiral of CTE. He provides us with a compassionate, personal, and honest account of his brother's struggle with the outward manifestations of changes to parts of the brain with such names as amygdala, hippocampus, orbitofrontal cortex, diencephalon, and brain stem.

We all need this glimpse through the window into the real world of someone struggling with this brain disease. We hear about it on the news whenever a professional football player dies of suicide. We watch documentaries about "the concussion crisis," or leagues in denial. We see prime-time television shows attempting to depict cases of CTE through the eyes of TV lawyers, doctors, or forensic specialists. At the water cooler, there are discussions about the future of football. There has been tremendous hype about this brain disease, and yet, very little is really known. In this book, Jim Proebstle's description of his brother shows the devastation of CTE to us all—doctors, scientists, sports fans, everyone. It's a beautiful description of this complex disease that transcends the simplistic descriptions portrayed in the media and in scientific publications.

CTE is a neurodegenerative disease that is similar to, but distinct from, Alzheimer's disease. It has been found most often in professional athletes involved in contact sports (e.g., boxing, American football, rugby, ice hockey) and subjected to repetitive blows to the head, including those resulting in concussions or even asymptomatic, "subconcussive" trauma. We have known about it since the early twentieth century, when it was first referred to as "punch-drunk syndrome" or "dementia pugilistica," because it was thought to occur only in boxers. Neuropathologically confirmed CTE has been reported in individuals as young as seventeen and in contact sport athletes who played sports only through high school or college, such as Dick Proebstle. Moreover, CTE has been found in nonathletes who have experienced multiple head impacts, including individuals with epilepsy, developmentally disabled individuals with histories of head banging, and victims of physical abuse. Recently, CTE has been neuropathologically diagnosed in members of the armed services who had been deployed in Iraq and Afghanistan and have histories of repetitive brain trauma.

All cases of neuropathologically confirmed CTE reported to date have had a history of repetitive head impacts, indicating that the head trauma may be a necessary variable for the initiation of the cascade of events that take place in the brain that eventually leads to neurodegeneration. However, those blows to the head are obviously not a sufficient variable; that is, not everyone who gets their head hit a lot develops this brain disease. Symptoms begin years or decades following exposure to the head impacts and include changes in cognition, mood, behavior, and, in some people, motor problems. As the disease progresses, it can lead to dementia. Unfortunately, CTE, like most other neurodegenerative diseases, can only be definitively diagnosed postmortem.

So many unanswered questions remain about this disease: How common is it? Why does one person get it and another does not? What are the additional risk factors or prevention factors, such as genetics? How can we treat it? How can it be prevented? To answer those questions, our research group and other investigators around the globe are now developing methods of diagnosing the disease during life. It is our hope that with appropriate and early detection and diagnosis, we will eventually be able to develop effective treatments for CTE that could be initiated early in the course of the disease. This would lead to the ability to help countless individuals, such as Dick Proebstle, while they are still alive and before they and their loved ones suffer from the devastating changes associated with this disease. It is only through courageous and selfless individuals such as the Proebstle family that we can reach this goal. Through postmortem brain donation and through research participation during life of those at risk for CTE, we will make tremendous gains in our efforts to treat and, ultimately, prevent CTE.

Robert A. Stern, PhD
Professor of Neurology, Neurosurgery and
Anatomy and Neurobiology
Clinical Core Director, Boston University Alzheimer's
Disease and CTE Center
Boston University School of Medicine
Boston, Massachusetts
February 2015

INTRODUCTION

Unintended Impact: One Athlete's Journey from Concussions in Amateur Football to CTE Dementia is a very personal story about two brothers—how one brother looked out for his younger brother early in life and how those roles were reversed later in life. My brother Dick and I grew up in America's hotbed of high school football, in Massillon and Canton, Ohio, during the '50s and '60s. In some respects, we are caricatures of thousands of boys and men who love football, enjoyed the benefits of having played, and experienced its residual impact throughout life.

Dick, my older brother by two years and the middle son in our family, was an aging athlete and competitive business opportunist who struggled unknowingly with Chronic Traumatic Encephalopathy (CTE) dementia. He fought the demons of a life trapped in a world of diminished short-term memory, limited executive functioning, deepening interpersonal shortcomings, and failed physical capabilities. Dick clung to a vision of achievement in sports and business as his only bridge between his world of dementia and his past. As an athlete, he was revered; yet, success turned traitor as the concussions received in football led to a world of confusion, poor decision-making, and confinement defined by a wheelchair in a long-term care facility. In his multiple levels of impaired functioning, the opportunity for Dick to "get it"—life, that is—was over. He just didn't know it. My wife, Carole, and I, along with Dick's son and daughter, attempted to reassemble the carnage left at the

1

intersection of Dick's CTE dementia, his need to be validated, and his life events.

Nobody will remember a backup college quarterback, but Dick's story bridges the glamour of NFL football—its high-profile athletes and its $765 million settlement for players with CTE dementia—and the millions of anonymous amateur football players who may suffer with the same concussion-induced devastation of CTE dementia. *Unintended Impact* makes a statement to be vigilant about the clinical diagnostic criteria, or what I call the markers, of CTE. They may appear earlier in life than expected as a result of the dings and bell-ringing episodes taken for granted in many sports where collision impact to the head can cause traumatic brain injuries. Dick Proebstle's story covers the drama from childhood to adulthood, including numerous personal and business episodes that serve as warnings that something had been derailed. In 2015, with today's focus on CTE, lack of knowledge is not acceptable. Yet in Dick's life, lack of knowledge was just one of the underlying factors contributing to the heartbreak of his tragedy. With the vast number of amateur athletes who play or have played football or other contact sports, the question needs to be asked: How many other Dick Proebstles are there?

In relating this creative nonfiction memoir account, there were numerous challenges to "not pull any punches," so I regret the inevitable offense and possible insult I may have generated by exposing the truth as I experienced it. My mother put it nicely many years ago when talking about truth and the possibility of offending people. She said, "That's why God gave people toes." If I stepped on yours, it was for the story's greater purpose. Knowledge has a way of revising our memories and thinking, and that's certainly what happened when we discovered the truth of CTE. CBS uses three criteria for newsworthy reporting: "Is it right? Is it fair? And is it honest?" That made sense to me in presenting this story. It was my goal to utilize the same standard of frankness, no matter how difficult the situation and regardless of whom it affected, including myself.

CHAPTER 1

"How did this happen?"
I said to no one, my head down,
resting in both hands.

"Bad men! Coming after me! Hid . . . under the boat," Dick said, desperately struggling with the formation of each word. His eyes were wild, displaying terror, as he continued in his confusion. "They grabbed me . . . tied me down. They are bad men . . . you know, from the south side."

"Where are you, Dick? The south side of where?"

I had witnessed Dick's descent into dementia for several years and could generally make out the halting dialogue peppered with disconnected sentences and nouns. Much guesswork was needed from a listener's point of view, but to Dick, his rants had very specific meaning. Word retrieval was painstaking for Dick—for me, as well. Brothers have a way of filling in the blanks, though, especially when they are so close. Today, however, Dick's heightened emotions led to tremendous agitation in his efforts to talk.

"South Canton! Steel mills," he said as if it should have been obvious. "They're trying to get me. I hid . . . under the boat!"

Dick's frustration in not making his point was matched by his determined tone of accomplishment in avoiding capture. He was reclined in his La-Z-Boy lift chair in the nursing home room, half covered with his blanket—sweat lightly covering the upper half of his body. The parkinsonian shaking of his hands waving in punctuation to his achievement of "hiding" accelerated his sense of fear.

"Elevator . . . bright lights . . . I had to hang on . . ."

All of this was in response to one question I asked, inquiring about Dick's recent trip to the hospital from the Peabody, an adult independent- and assisted-living center in North Manchester, Indiana. The Peabody's staff had found him late the previous night in a very nonresponsive condition, sitting in bed, but not really able to communicate with or take any direction from the nurse about going back to sleep. The paramedics were called, and he was rushed via ambulance to a small hospital in North Manchester, Indiana, south of Warsaw, where Dick's son, Mike, lived.

Normally, I could understand Dick's jumbled and limited conversations, but I struggled to find the logic that was so clear to Dick. I was tired from the drive from Chicago. *Maybe,* I thought, *it's me. Somehow, I'm just not connecting.*

As we sat next to Dick, it was Carole, my wife of forty-nine years and an accomplished psychologist, who finally put the pieces together after the ten minutes or so of Dick's stream of consciousness dialogue.

"The 'bad men' were probably the 911 response team members who came to move him from his room here at the Peabody to the hospital. And seeing we're on the first floor here, the 'elevator' had to be at the hospital. It's possible the safety straps securing him to the gurney were, in his fragile state, 'ropes' tying him down. The 'boat' he hid under could have easily been the MRI unit for his CAT scan. It must have been very scary and disorienting for him with all the lights, the response team grabbing him, the movement of the gurney, and the ambulance ride with the blaring siren all the while."

What Carole said made sense. I sat there and massaged Dick's tight shoulders and took in the plain room at the Peabody. While the facility's outside layout resembled a small Midwest college campus, the aesthetics inside added little for Dick. At one point, Dick had owned a seventeen-thousand-square-foot home, immaculately appointed. And now all his worldly possessions fit comfortably in this colorless, 150-square-foot room with enough space only for two bookshelves to display some memorabilia from a pretty amazing life. To the staff's credit, however, the room was kept very clean and without the telltale smell of urine common in elder-care facilities.

"Something's happened," Carole said. "Maybe a stroke. But he's definitely experienced an event that has dropped his capacity off the cliff, and he's not able to recognize things as being real or not any longer."

Her years of objective observation as a staff psychologist at Oak Forest Hospital in Chicago were reflected in her unemotional demeanor and comments. There she had dealt with a wide variety of patients with neurological disorders, from individuals with strokes to those suffering from the chronic effects of traumatic brain injuries, street crimes, and gunshots. The cerebral cortex, or gray matter, can be damaged in all these scenarios, and it plays an important role in memory, attention, awareness, thought, language, and consciousness.

I sat there quietly for some time as Carole gently brought Dick back to the current reality of his long-term care room at the Peabody. Dick was only sixty-nine—a powerful man with a very solid 220-pound, six-foot-two frame—but the childlike terror I saw in his eyes was new.

"Were you afraid?" I asked.

"Yeah." Dick nodded vigorously. "I was."

"Everything is okay now," I said, putting my hand on Dick's forearm for reassurance.

All of this hit me right in the gut, as he had never been afraid of anything. He was a phenomenal athlete in both high school and college and a successful entrepreneur in the construction equipment industry, owning a Clark Equipment dealership, well known for its Bobcat product line. Dick had risen above fear, always facing challenges head on and never really accepting that something couldn't be done. *And besides, Dick was my big brother, always looking out for me,* I thought. Now I saw a terrified child reacting to a bogeyman dream sequence and not being able to reconcile his reality after waking up.

"How did this happen?" I said to no one, my head down, resting in both hands.

"As I said," Carole answered, "it may have been a stroke complicated by the—"

"No, I mean, how did he get here from where he was?" I interrupted.

My rhetorical question was followed by our silence as we looked at Dick, at the absent expression, the vacancy overshadowing any meaningful understanding of events as Dick drifted into a temporary stupor.

"Do you think he's able to process his mental decline from just a few years ago?" I asked.

CHAPTER 1

It hadn't been but a short time since Dick was moved to the long-term care unit of the Peabody. His decline accelerated faster than any of us had expected: two months in independent care, five months in assisted living, one month in rehab with a broken hip, and now here. Previous to the Peabody were two unsuccessful attempts at living with his kids—Patty in Newtown, Pennsylvania, and Mike in Warsaw, Indiana.

Carole returned my look with an expression of hopelessness, shaking her head, confirming my fear that nobody really knew. She shrugged as she said, "Maybe it's been a lot more than two years."

"The white box . . . the white box," Dick said, jerking himself awake while sitting in his tilt chair. "In the room," he said, pointing with purpose toward the sterile bathroom.

I looked quickly and found nothing resembling a white box, so I asked Carole to look. She saw nothing that would match Dick's need. We asked the nurse, and she was equally as perplexed.

"The 'white box' is probably something in his mind, maybe from the past or a part of his dysfunctional imagination—although it could just as easily be the toilet," Carole said as the aromatic emergence of soiled Depends permeated the air. "We'll see more of this with his loss of mental functioning." Carole's experience had her much more prepared for Dick's circumstances than I was.

At that moment, Dick began bringing our attention to Carole's black winter boots with a shaking hand that pointed emphatically. His eyes widened as if to express a newfound thought, but his attempt to verbalize his discovery passed. In frustration, and maybe in a feeling of loss, his head fell to his chest. The photographs and memorabilia that represented his life—family, Canton Central Catholic, Michigan State, and his business—didn't matter anymore. He was no longer really here.

* * *

On our drive back to Chicago that evening, Carole and I recounted Dick's rise and fall throughout life in disbelief, as if the conversation was new to us. Then we both retreated into silence as the snow-covered road passed in the darkness.

Many athletes achieve Dick's level of success in high school, only to not reach full athletic potential in college. Many college graduates don't make the grade in law school. Many people divorce; fewer divorce twice. Many fathers have a disenfranchised relationship with their children. And while there are many wealthy independent business entrepreneurs, few have ended life in poverty. Few men, however, have lived through the misfortune of all these outcomes. Dick was one. *It's inconceivable that Dick brought all this on himself,* I thought with absolute conviction. He had too much going on that was positive. The injustice defied logic.

"He brought some of this on himself," Carole suddenly said as if she had read my mind.

"Maybe, but not everything. It's just sad. I feel less sure now than ever that we have all the facts," I said. "I mean, when did you first recognize something was wrong?"

It was late, and the solitude as we drove across rural portions of US Route 30 in northern Indiana seemed to be the perfect tonic to ease the words out.

She reflected for a minute. "You remember the night

before your dad died? He told me something was wrong with Dick. That was over twenty years ago. Do you think this was what he meant?"

I too reflected for a brief moment before responding. "Hard to say. Except for the last few years, we haven't been around Dick enough to judge. I guess it depends on whether Dad was talking about physiology or psychology—or maybe both. God knows there's plenty to chew on, regardless."

It was January 2012, and a few articles about CTE dementia were just beginning to reveal the brain damage from multiple concussions suffered in collision sports. While evidence and research wasn't yet definitive, the notoriety of NFL players—some of whom had even committed suicide—certainly seemed to raise a red flag. As a quarterback and linebacker in the '50s and '60s, Dick had incurred more concussions than most—so much so that he was tormented by migraines throughout adulthood.

As for interpersonal development, Dick had succeeded in pushing away many people who spent time around him, not because he was a bad person, however. Carole had a saying that "strengths used in excess can become weaknesses." Dick's competitiveness never left him and had turned into an outward attitude of superiority. His self-confidence could easily be seen as arrogance, and his need for praise was probably what led him to seek out friends who would give it. In many cases, these friends were people who seemed to see Dick as their gateway to his status and money, who seemed to use his need for recognition to fulfill their own purposes.

"I don't know if we'll be in the car long enough to flush this one out, honey," I said. "I mean, we're talking about a lifetime."

As we drifted again into silence, I thought back to the first time I realized Dick might be different.

It was my big day as an incoming freshman at Central Catholic. Dick had convinced me to bypass freshman football and try out for the varsity team. That was huge, because in Canton and Massillon in the late '50s, high school football pretty much ranked ahead of sex and independent wealth on Maslow's hierarchy of needs. Baby boys in that area of Ohio were given footballs instead of rattles. The line between the Massillon Tigers and the Canton McKinley Bulldogs was drawn right down the middle, between neighbors, churchgoers, and coworkers. Our high school, Central Catholic, was right in between, but not even on the map football-wise.

"Jimmy," Dick had said, "varsity is the way to go . . . skip the freshman crap."

Even though I liked being called Jim best, Dick called me Jimmy. I guess it was a snot-nosed kid brother name.

To top things off, Dick was single-handedly one of the best athletes in the county—and likely the state. He had six varsity letters in football, basketball, and baseball going into his junior year. This was a big deal. He was on track to receive twelve high school varsity letters in the three major sports—something that had never been done in Ohio. And nothing to turn your nose up at, because nationally, Stark County was considered the heart of the best high school football, with outstanding athletes in every other sport as well.

There's no question I was a victim of my big brother's expectations when I tried out as a freshman. Even though I ultimately made the team and developed some skills, on that first day, I got killed by the older and more developed players.

CHAPTER 1

I had a revelation about Dick as I left the field and encountered our star running back, John Brown. I heard his voice as I was turning the corner where the chain-link fence separated the field from a unique grotto where one could commemorate the stations of the cross. I hadn't really met John until then.

"You're not going to be like your brother, are you?" were his first words to me.

I was just fourteen and only vaguely knew what he meant. He didn't say it as a compliment.

"What do you mean?" I asked back, continuing my direction to the locker room. I was so tired that if I stopped walking, I knew it would be an effort to just stand there.

"You know, like you think you're better than everyone else," was his answer.

My instinct was to say Dick *was* better than everyone else, but I didn't. There seemed to be an underlying meaning to John's comment. Over the years, his words played over and over in my mind as a metaphor for Dick's struggle to handle success.

A mild sleet began, and the windshield wiper noise helped me enter back into our conversation.

"Dick was probably a little over-the-top for most people around him to understand. Carole, when I say he was good at everything, I mean everything: Cub Scouts, Boy Scouts, Explorer Scouts, altar boy, choir, community service, student council, and a permanent member on the honor roll and National Honor Society. Let alone athletics."

"What made him so good? It's not like he was super-human and wore a cape," Carole broke in. She knew I felt Dick was one of the best athletes I had ever played with in high school or college.

"There were so many factors that came into play. It's hard to say," I responded while entering the on-ramp to I-65 north.

"Maybe if you just broke your thoughts down into smaller buckets," she said.

It was hard to begin. For one, he was a man-child . . . with brains. Hell, he had to bring his birth certificate to Little League baseball games because the opposing teams' parents refused to believe he was only twelve and were fearful for their kids. He was six-foot-two and a 190 pounds . . . and shaved.

One time he hit a batter in the head with a wild pitch and knocked the poor kid unconscious on top of home plate, lying face first in the dust. I thought the kid was dead; the parents went berserk. The ambulance came, and the game was canceled. I knew Dick's reaction wasn't normal when he unemotionally rationalized it days later in practice: "It was the batter's job to get out of the way of a bad pitch."

"You know how most kids feel bad when they hurt other kids?" I asked as I relayed the story. "But Carole, it never bothered him. Dick may have had a mean streak—or was just being hard-nosed, as we used to say."

When we went on family road trips to Minnesota, we would stop for lunch at roadside parks. We'd be out of the car immediately, peeing in the weeds and playing hardball catch—in that order. But *catch* for Dick was different—"burn," he called it. That ball came so fast that if you caught it in the palm of the glove, you would dance in agony. Everyone was afraid to bat against Dick, and that definitely included me.

We started grade school football in the fifth grade. The weight limit for running backs was 125 pounds, so our coach, Joe Guanieri, played Dick at linebacker. Just about every time he intercepted a pass, he ran it back for a touch-down. He was scary.

"Truth is," I said, "he set the bar high early on and was obsessed with being the best, no matter if it was football, the classroom, whatever. He expected you to measure up or get run over. It made me feel good to be his brother. Back then, boys were expected to be tough."

"Did your parents intervene?" Carole asked. "I mean, it's likely that this hypercompetitiveness was masking some inner need."

"Sure, on some occasions. But I think it was a difficult work-in-progress for them too. Imagine, here's your kid: All-Everything in the three major sports while receiving student-of-the-month awards from the Canton *Repository* newspaper. Combined with the National Honor Society and student council, I think my parents were so busy being proud that they might have missed some early development signs. Wouldn't you?" I asked, looking over at her. "Do you think that's what Dad meant with his comment about Dick? Or maybe there's more?"

The congestion of trucks and merging lanes and the grittiness of the weather interrupted my thinking and our conversation as we transitioned onto I-80 west, south of Chicago. My dad wasn't one to make a comment without the facts. *But those facts were buried with him and Mom years ago,* I thought as I crossed another lane of traffic.

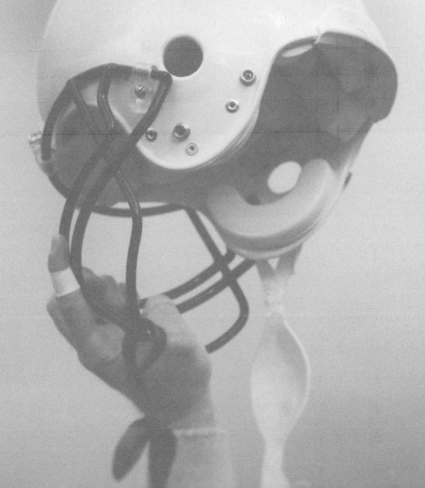

SECTION I

CTE ORIGIN—YOUR CONCUSSIONS BEGIN

CHAPTER 2

*Most of us started
tackle football at age ten.*

When we were growing up, Doc Emmel was the family dentist who always had a few words to say about football when Dick and I made our semiannual visit. His bushy eyebrows and deep dimples gave him a friendly appearance. It's hard to know whether he was trying to distract us from our overwhelming fear of the drill or whether he was genuinely interested in our growing talents in football. He was very involved with the Massillon Tiger Booster Club in the late '50s and early '60s and an avid fan of high school football.

His dental practice was located in the front rooms of his stately white Victorian home just across the Tuscarawas River in Massillon. *He must be rich,* I thought as I approached the house, but all of that left me when the fear-producing smell of clover and other volatile solvents hit once we entered his office.

"It's a shame you boys aren't playing for the Tigers," he said. "With your size and talent, both of you would make the team easily."

Doc didn't come out and say it, but there was a growing

concern among Tigers fans that Central was elevating their game quickly under Coach John McVay. McVay had been an All-State center for Massillon High and a Little All-American for Miami of Ohio. As a resident of Massillon and coming out of Miami—nicknamed the "Cradle of Coaches," with names such as Paul Brown, Woody Hayes, Weeb Ewbank, Sid Gillman, Ara Parseghian, Bo Schembechler, and Johnny Pont to their coaching credit—McVay's appointment as Central's head coach in 1956 had locals taking notice. Ultimately, Coach McVay would go on to be an assistant coach for the Michigan State Spartans, head coach for the Dayton Flyers, head coach for the Memphis Southmen of the World Football League, and head coach for the New York Giants. He also earned five Super Bowl rings as the general manager for the 49ers working with head coach Bill Walsh. Little did they realize how concerned they should be.

"You boys thank Doc Emmel for the compliment," Dad said.

"Thanks, Doc," we replied politely in unison.

The truth was, neither of us could think much about football when staring at the praying mantis-like, medieval drill we were about to endure. And if that wasn't enough, the size of the Novocain needle was just about cause to pee our pants. Football was easy compared to Doc Emmel.

"That might have been the case," Dad continued, "had their mother not been so insistent on a Catholic education. She's a McDermott, you know, and those Irish Catholics are pretty set in their ways when it comes to the Lord." Dad was a converted Catholic and could distance himself from the theology when the conversation dictated—but never around Mom and definitely not around our grandmother.

She would have eviscerated him.

Doc was just one of many Massillon High booster club caricatures who lived and died with high school football. Massillon and Canton had a predominantly blue-collar employment base in steel and industry that fed right into the Friday night football rivalries between the many like-minded communities making up northeast Ohio. Baseball was king as a professional sport in America, but you wouldn't know it in this part of the country. The area was forever labeled the heart and home of football, important to the history of the NFL. In the early days of football, there were three local professional franchises, one each in Massillon, Canton, and Akron. The legendary Jim Thorpe played for the Canton Bulldogs. Football was the bedrock of the culture, and it naturally handed down to the high school level. In Massillon and Canton, the high schools gave their offensive schemes to the respective youth programs—nobody showed up as a freshman unprepared.

Within the Diocese of Youngstown, which covered Canton and Massillon, was an extremely well-developed network of Catholic grade schools with well-coached and organized football leagues as well. They were beginning to challenge the big public school systems in terms of preparation with most of us starting tackle football at age ten.

Catholic or not, if you grew up in Massillon, you were always in the shadow of Tiger Stadium, a twenty-thousand-seat, concrete high school stadium serving a town of about twenty-five thousand. You couldn't buy a pack of gum on Friday night during football season, as most stores were closed with a schedule and a "Go, Tigers" sign on the door. Each Tiger game and score was carefully marked on the poster by the proprietor.

In grade school, we lived close to the stadium and mostly went to the Tiger games, as Central wasn't on the map yet. It was in the parking lot during halftime that, at the age of twelve, I learned to smoke and drink coffee with my friends Tim and Bill. The adults always looked cool to me, with their cigarettes and paper cups of steaming coffee—*staying warm during the game,* I thought. Dick never participated with us. He was two years older and stuck with my parents and oldest brother, John, during the game. From the beginning, he seemed to enjoy following the rules better than anyone else. I represented the opposite end of the bell curve when it came to rules. But football always remained our link as brothers—we loved everything about the game.

Our dad's background as an aeronautical engineer at Goodyear Aerospace put him in a unique league of talented engineers—white short-sleeved shirts, plastic pocket protectors, mechanical pencils, and all—designing ballistic missile guidance systems with slide rules. We never knew this at the time, only that his work was top secret. All we saw was a very intelligent, disciplined, and principled father. His attention to detail was not lost on us, as every opportunity for our improvement was vocalized—with his best intentions, I truly believe, but it was nonetheless demanding. His strong German upbringing in Minnesota was not skipping a generation on his watch either. The strictness almost broke my older brother John, who was two years older than Dick. Being firstborn isn't always the best of strategies, not that he had a choice in the matter. Dad loved all of us from the bottom of his heart, and we were going to be the best at whatever we did, regardless.

The balancing offset was the love and encouragement from our mother. If he was strict, she was more dutiful, always looking for what was right and good and ready to acknowledge us with praise. Pleasing both of them was a rare accomplishment, but rewarding when it happened. Ultimately, I believe this motivation was a deep-seated psychological driver for Dick, the middle child.

* * *

We moved to a terrific house at Lake Cable in the fall of 1957, when I was in eighth grade. It was right on the lake with an acre of grass and a basketball court in the driveway. Our house became the place where most of our friends gathered. The court layout was almost half that of a regular court, with enough room for a five-on-five game. You just didn't want to miss the pass back out to the top of the court; otherwise, the ball would go right into the lake.

After sneaking a few cigarettes with a friend down the street one Saturday morning, I returned home right before lunch and entered directly from a kitchen side door. I could smell the aroma of simmering bean soup on the stove to the left as I entered. While the homemade flowered curtains generally added a cheery attitude to the room, today was not one of those days. My entry was poorly timed.

Dick was pinned in the corner of the kitchen dining area at the table. His face was blotchy, and he had been crying. Mom and Dad were severely chastising him for something. I knew it was bad, at least in their minds, as they rarely tag-teamed us kids.

Instantly, I heard my dad say, "That's no way to treat your older brother! He may not have your talents in sports, but that's no reason to make him look foolish."

This was not a new topic, as *family* was an important value in our home. Our parents were of Midwest upbringing with an old-school "you're-not-better-than-anyone-else" value system. Excellence and overachievement were expected, but you'd better not display it in an attitude of superiority.

Mom was crying with disappointment—the entire scene was up for grabs. "You let down the whole family when you do this," she said, "and it's just not fair to John." Her calico-print apron was knotted in her hands in frustration. Used, balled-up Kleenexes were on the Formica tabletop.

"You're making your mother cry with this behavior," Dad interjected while standing over Dick, dishing out the guilt.

"I'm sorry. I really am," came the half-muffled apology through his tears.

Dad and Mom had apparently been at it for a time, judging from Dick's emotional state, and they had likely impressed upon him how mean and unbrotherly his behavior had been. I knew from my own experiences as the younger brother that when Dick's competitive juices kicked in, there was no stopping him. For the most part, his competitiveness only raised my game; that wasn't the case with John.

It didn't matter that Dick was a sophomore and John a senior. John just didn't have the athletic skills Dick had. Too often, Dick would run roughshod over John when others were around—today it had been on our driveway basketball court.

John was nowhere to be found in the house—probably decided to clear out when the incident exploded. I passed through the kitchen like a ghost and out of the line of fire. I probably smelled like an ashtray and sure didn't want their wrath turned on me. My parents definitely did not condone smoking.

I never did find out exactly what happened. Maybe it was sibling rivalry and just part of brothers being brothers. But with each instance, John just shrank further into the background. It may have been that Dick was living up to our dad's expectation of the firstborn male, knowing he could and John could not.

I also think Dad was extra harsh on Dick because of the circumstances surrounding the loss of his only brother, Curly, during World War II. Curly was a pilot for Northwest Airlines when he joined the Air Transport Command, flying for the US Army. His plane crashed on Mount Deception in Alaska with three crew and sixteen passengers on board. The search-and-rescue team never found the bodies, despite finding a relatively intact wreckage site. It never made sense, and it took a hard toll on Dad. He and Curly had been tight and shared a passion for flying. They did everything together as young men growing up in Staples, Minnesota. The picture of Curly on my dad's chest of drawers in the master bedroom was a constant reminder and probably the catalyst for tremendous disappointment in Dick's behavior. This was not the way brothers should be treating each other. Dick even looked like Curly.

"Now go find your brother and apologize," Mom said, still gripping the homemade apron. She had stopped crying. "You can be better than this."

"You have a basketball game tonight," Dad added, "and I want you two to play as part of a team . . . understood?"

Dick's body language was nonresponsive, partly as a

result of trying to restore his composure.

"Do you understand, I said. I want an answer!" Dad was *always* understood, and we all knew that silence was never an answer when Dad wanted a confirmation.

"Yes, I understand," Dick responded feebly.

Inside, I knew he wanted to do the right thing, yet that air of superior competitiveness was often hard to control.

John scored a personal best with twelve points for Central that night, and Dick had six assists. My parents were happy.

CHAPTER 3

*One of the assistant coaches
had some smelling salts that helped
clear our heads after vicious hits.*

My first remembrance of a Central home game was as an eighth grader in 1958 when the Crusaders played Akron's Archbishop Hoban Knights on a clear fall Friday night—classic high school football in Ohio with a fired-up, capacity home crowd of over seven thousand. The smells of popcorn, coffee, soda, hot dogs, and cigarette smoke combined with the sound of leather pads smacking as the players made contact on the field.

Central's win included a thirty-five-yard Hail Mary pass from Dick to John Wachtel, our All-Conference end. Time ran out after a perfectly orchestrated drive covering most of the field. The crowd went wild. It was a big win for Central; people were starting to notice. Even the new stadium, with its unique serpentine brick wall design, spoke to a team on the rise.

After the game, one of the players' parents hosted a party for the other parents, which opened the door for the players to have unauthorized parties at the vacated homes.

Mike Fay, Dick's best friend since grade school, and his date wanted to double with Dick and his girlfriend, Jane Matthews—a cute blonde Central majorette.

Dick objected. "You know I don't want to be around drinking. I don't need beer to get high. But if I only drink orange juice, people say I'm boring and don't know how to have fun. We don't need them."

"Can't we just stop for a while?" Jane pleaded. "We don't have to stay long. I'd really like to see everyone. C'mon—it'll be fun."

Jane was proud to be seen with Dick because of the attention she got as well. She lived next door to Coach McVay and was very popular. She and Dick made for an envious couple, yet they never really warmed up to the other popular couples—just to a few non-jocks who worshiped Dick because he had everything they didn't. To say he was their idol was not overstating their relationship. The other players and girlfriends, however, backed away from Dick.

Mike, one of Dick's true friends, was indifferent about Dick's objection to the party. But Dick relented to Jane's wishes, and they all went.

"With everyone drinking, it's hard to talk," Dick said soon after their arrival, furthering his objection. It wasn't long before the two couples went their separate ways that evening.

Dick's social skills lagged in maturity, causing him to talk only about what he knew best—himself. "They can't carry my jock," he told me more than once, referring to the other players and his somewhat self-serving attitude for "having to do everything" for a win. He believed that if it weren't for him, the team would probably lose. While his teammates would likely agree, they didn't appreciate his sense of superiority. And when they did lose, Jane spent the evening consoling Dick, as he sometimes cried, bemoaning that it was all his "fault" and that it was he who had lost the game. As much as Jane tried to tell him he wasn't the only player on the field, Dick believed he made the team what it was—and achieving the brass ring was everything for Dick.

In the classroom, on the field, with other parents, in extracurricular activities, and in school leadership, though, he did excel. In reality, he was simply a step ahead of most of his classmates. His struggle with his own success prevented him from developing a lighthearted side that could open the door to having fun—at least, the caliber of fun matching a high school mentality. His insistence on not drinking was probably a way to hold himself to a higher benchmark, and most of us would have agreed, as he simply did have higher standards.

He ultimately did want peer acceptance, but the more he tried to impress people with his accomplishments— which were naturally bigger and better than everyone else's—the more he pushed people away. Instinctively, Dick fell back on his dominant talent, competitiveness, when trying to make friends. In his mind, he thought, *If you don't like me, I'll give you more to be impressed with, and then you'll certainly like me. How could this not be the right approach?*

"I don't really need the parties . . . I just like being with you," Dick told Jane later. They were parked at a quiet location near the Pony League baseball field not far from our home in Crescent Gardens in Massillon. "I'll give you a quarter to sit closer to me," Dick teased, making a contest out of necking.

The fall air held a slight chill, and the night was perfect for her to agree. They were quiet for several moments, Dick with his arm around Jane as she snuggled close on the bench seat of the four-door family Buick. WHKK was playing "Kisses Sweeter than Wine" by Jimmie Rodgers. He could feel her breasts against his side, which triggered the "near occasion of sin" concept the Christian Brothers had drilled into our thinking at Central Catholic. Dick wouldn't allow himself to cross that line.

As a distraction, Dick proposed to her out of nowhere in a half-serious tone. "Why don't we get married and join the Ice Capades?" Jane and Dick were both very skilled on figure skates, but this proposal was a little bizarre, even to Jane. Unfortunately, this naïve, almost simplistic side of Dick colored their relationship.

In the months to come, Jane soon began thinking of Dick more as a brother. They weren't ready to move forward—at least, he wasn't, anyway, she concluded. After the prom that year, they broke up, and she started dating someone else.

"He can't give you the things I can," Dick said, voicing his objection. "High school will be over, and I'll have a scholarship to any school I want."

But Jane moved on, as did Dick, who began dating Diane Demont right after the breakup. Some thought Diane was using Dick, but those views were probably just high school jealousy. Diane was also a Central majorette, but it was her voice that Dick fell in love with. He loved music. She had a Julie Andrews's look and style that made her the envy of every girl in her class. She would solo in front of the whole school with a flawless "Ave Maria" performance along with holiday songs at the Christmas assembly. In person, she was comfortable to be with—maybe a little shy. But on stage, she was a dynamo.

CHAPTER 3

* * *

Dick began his senior year in fall of 1959, and Central's football team was on a roll. Two-a-day practices during the August heat and humidity were as tough as I ever remember, including those later on in college. You could always tell when two-a-days were ready to start just by the distinct musty smell of the grass in the fall air.

John McVay was a fair coach, but tough. Dick played quarterback and linebacker. In those days, all teams were governed by rules that prohibited the unlimited substitution of players. Part of the logic was to prevent the bigger schools from having an unfair advantage over their smaller rivals. As a consequence, a coach had to keep his best players on the field playing "both ways," and that meant every play of the game if you expected to win. The only break you'd get during practice or a game was on a time-out, with just enough time to suck dirty water out of a soaked towel from a bucket that forty to fifty players shared. We called it the "slop bucket," with its mixture of sweat, dirt, and water. On those hot August days, however, it tasted like salvation.

"Men, I want you to know this team will never be beaten by a team in better condition."

McVay always said this right before a segment of practice when we thought we would die. Sometimes it was wind sprints, maybe an extended full-contact scrimmage, or perhaps drills to toughen us up. Today, we would "learn how to tackle." But standing around watching Coach McVay demonstrate the drill was the only breather we'd get, so we liked that.

"You see these numbers on the jersey? They're there for a reason . . . they're your target. I want you to put your hat"—his word for helmet—"right on these numbers and drive through with your legs. Jimmy, what's the strongest muscle in the body?" he asked me so everyone could hear.

"The neck, Coach," I answered, as I had been trained.

"That's right. So you're not going to hurt yourself when you make the tackle correctly."

He crouched in an athletic stance—he wasn't a big man at 150 pounds—and showed us exactly what he wanted, demonstrating at half speed on one of the players as a dummy.

"But you've got to hit like a truck and drive. When you do it right, you'll pick the runner up, squeeze your arms around his legs—like this—and deposit him flat on his back."

With that, the player involved in the role play was driven into the ground, flat on his back, with the clear sound of the helmet smacking the hard turf from the accelerated force.

"You see what happens when you hit with the head first, don't you?" he said rhetorically to the group. "Correll, what follows the head?"

Bruce Correll was an offensive lineman and close friend of mine. He was taken somewhat off guard by the coach's question. He shuffled his feet but didn't have an answer.

Coach brought Bruce in front of the group. "Now, Correll, tell me what this is called," he said, gesturing to Bruce's torso. "If you get this wrong, you'll get an F in my class."

McVay also taught sophomore biology. Many of his lessons came as crossover metaphors. He had a great way of loosening up the team when he often needed to.

"The body?" Bruce said, slightly confused.

"Do you have a girlfriend, Correll?"

The team knew this would be good.

"Yes, Coach, I do," Bruce said, trying to muster some confidence.

McVay put his arm around Bruce's shoulders and said, "I know you're just fifteen, but it's important that you are absolutely convinced this is your body. In time, she'll want you to know that too."

Everybody laughed.

"I'm sure, Coach!" Bruce boomed.

"Good. There's hope for you after all. Now, the reason I want to make sure Correll here knows this is his body is because it can't go anywhere his head doesn't go. Isn't that right, Correll?"

"Yes, Coach," Bruce responded, wishing the lesson would end soon.

"Right again. That's why I want your hat right on these numbers when you tackle," Coach said, slapping Bruce forcefully in the center of his chest. "When you do that and drive your legs like I demonstrated, the full weight of your body becomes a weapon. Everybody understand? All right, now give me two lines. And you might as well get comfortable . . . we're going to be here awhile."

Coach McVay was an excellent fundamentals coach and knew our chances were better if we excelled at the basics. Over the next thirty minutes, the sounds of pads and leather hitting were intense as we paired up with our position partners. I was with Terry Clark, a 180-pound end. As I was much larger, we learned to cooperate and not try to kill each other. But still, it was like being tackled on concrete, especially when your helmet smacked the hard, dry ground. Looking back, I count myself lucky that year with Terry, as Alan Page became my tackling partner for the next two years.

Dick, at 200 pounds, was partnered with Ron Hoover, a 195-pound fullback and linebacker, possibly the toughest kid on the team. Both were powerful and skilled at driving their helmets right into the numbers as they made contact. And with powerful legs, they aggressively planted each other to the ground, just as Coach had demonstrated. Their aggressiveness set the tone for the drill as tempers escalated. Fighting would never be allowed on a McVay team, but that still left plenty of room for brutality as bodies were slammed into the turf, leaving some unable to get up right away. One of the assistant coaches had some smelling salts that helped clear our heads after vicious hits.

Originally, Congress mandated the use of a helmet to protect the skull. Over time, however, because of its newer hard shell, the helmet definitely became a weapon used to punish other players. Getting our "bell rung" was a natural by-product of those collisions. It was a "macho" part of the game.

What we didn't know was that the brain isn't really anchored to anything inside the skull. It floats in fluid. A sudden impact causes the brain to slosh around and slam against the inside the skull, much like a passenger inside a car during an accident. When this unintended impact happens, the injured brain calls out for more glucose, but the blood supply is compromised. In an attempt to get the chemistry back in balance, large quantities of potassium are released.

The result of the collision is fogginess, disorientation, and dizziness, sometimes accompanied with a brief blackout. Every player experiences them. I myself can remember three hits where I was either knocked out cold or got my bell rung. It was a strange, fuzzy feeling as I tried to regain composure. But the player in all of us wanted to push it aside and get back in the action. Otherwise, you felt as if you weren't tough enough, and maybe you were a little embarrassed.

"Punch-drunk" was a common term referring to boxers, but football coaches, doctors, and trainers didn't realize the potential brain damage caused by these aggressive collisions that resulted in concussions. A broken arm you could see—put on a cast and let it mend. The only "test" for a concussion that I can remember required the injured player to stand with heels together, hands at his sides, and eyes closed. If he lost balance, he might have a concussion. At which point, he would sit out for a few plays or at most a day, until he was "better."

The following twenty minutes were spent tackling from the side. "Your head needs to be in front of the runner, not behind," one of the position coaches yelled, correcting a player on how to avoid a broken arm tackle. "When your head is behind the runner, all you're tackling with is your arms. That's not good enough for the running backs we'll see. Now try it again."

This technique wasn't as dramatic as the head-on tackle, but the side impact left your head spinning when you made a mistake and caught the pumping thighs or knees of the runner.

The only short break came when that same assistant showed us a technique where the tackler would hold the runner up in place, giving another teammate a clear shot at the runner's lower back with the helmet. I found out later that some coaches referred to this technique as "spearing."

"Nail 'em to the cross," the assistant said, pointing to the kidney area. "We don't want you men playing dirty football, but we do want the other runners to know we're serious."

"We'll save that for the right time," Coach McVay intervened, steering the group's attention away from the assistant's lesson and back to the basics.

At the end of the drill, he said, "We're not going to be the biggest team on the field, but as long as I'm the coach, we will be the toughest. Good practice. And remember, we're in the classroom reviewing our playbooks at one o'clock and back on the field at two. Now, hit the showers. Take two more laps around the field before going in."

Dick knew, as a leader, he had to be first so the rest of the team could follow. He may have struggled developing friendships off the field, but on the field, Dick was "the man."

On the way back to the locker room, I saw McVay engaged with that same assistant, vigorously giving him some instructions. We never heard any more about the spearing technique in practice again. Later, I heard from my parents that the technique was outlawed in Ohio. Regardless, the expression "nail 'em to the cross" remained for years as a metaphor for a punishing tackle.

It wasn't uncommon to lose ten pounds in one practice session just from water loss. Before heading in for the classroom portion, we spent most of the two-hour break eating lunch and replenishing our fluids. We would consume literally gallons of Kool-Aid while resting in the shade of the campus trees. The canopy of the big hardwoods lowered the summer heat by five degrees—enough to make a difference.

McVay occasionally strolled through the area during these breaks. Recognizing our despair, he said, "Cheer up, boys—the worst is yet to come," referring to the second half of the two-a-day. The groans were real.

CHAPTER 3

We spent the classroom time reviewing our knowledge of position assignments. Each of us had a fifty-to-sixty-page mimeographed playbook we were expected to memorize. Each page had a separate play diagram. The quarterback was expected to know all plays for all positions. Coaches would pound the blackboards with their hands while scribbling Xs and Os to reinforce how the play would unfold. If you lost your playbook, your position on the team was in jeopardy, as the entire season could be at risk if it got into the hands of the opposition.

* * *

Everything the coaching staff preached to us boys that fall paid off, starting with a major victory over Saint Xavier. With this being the opener, both teams were amped up.

A key play of the game came early in the first quarter when Dick made a devastating fourth-down tackle as a linebacker in our 5-4 defense formation. He jammed the Xavier star fullback at the 5-yard line just as McVay had taught us—"put the hat right on the numbers and drive with the power of your legs." Dick's legs were exceptionally powerful, and the sound of leather was heard throughout the stadium, only to be instantaneously drowned out by the roar of the crowd.

Incidental to the play was the secondary collision of Dick's helmet in the scrum as it collided with their big offensive tackle's knee. Dick blacked out, but within seconds came to—dizzy, foggy, and disoriented.

"Are you all right?" Hoover said, noticing Dick's slowness getting up.

"Yeah, just give me a minute. I really got my bell rung!"

As Dick collected himself, both teams made a few quick substitutions. Surprisingly, Dick found himself standing in front of the huddle, ready to call a play, yet none came to mind. He shook his head to get the cobwebs out and called the one play he instinctively knew he could rely on—a quarterback sneak.

The previous year, Central had defeated the Ohio state championship team, Warren Harding, led by Paul Warfield, 8–0 in a night game at Warren, thanks to a quarterback sneak touchdown right after Dick got his bell rung. The second half of that game would be blurred from his memory for years to come. The quarterback sneak on a quick snap count had become the one play he knew he could count on when things got fuzzy, and it remained a favorite of Dick's. When he combined the power of his thighs and quickness of his feet with the talent of Central's All-County center, Norm Nicola, they were virtually guaranteed to pick up yards. Second down and five.

"That's a good call," McVay said to Coach Hanlon, the backfield coach.

"That's why we decided to have him call the plays . . . smart under pressure," Hanlon replied. "He's giving himself some room to work."

"Quarterback sneak on my sound," Dick said, calling the second play. It gained six yards. First down on the sixteen.

Now, with room to work, John Brown, Central's All-County halfback, was a logical selection for an off-tackle trap or sweep. But Dick said, "Quarterback sneak on my sound." Another four yards.

Coach McVay looked at Coach Hanlon with a questioning expression, but both had tremendous confidence in Dick and did not intervene.

Only after six straight quarterback sneaks and three first downs did Dick start remembering his playbook. He had operated out of pure muscle memory. It seemed brilliant to the fans, as Central now had reversed a negative field position and had the ball on the 42-yard line. The rest of the game played itself out beautifully, with Brown averaging fourteen yards per carry and rushing for two touchdowns and Dick firing a bullet TD pass to John Wachtel. Central victory!

"Great game, Dick. Good choice on the sneaks to settle the team down and get field position," Coach Hanlon said in the locker room.

Dick knew that playing hurt was part of the game and his role as a leader. The coach's comment reinforced his own decision to stay in, even though he couldn't remember most of the game.

Shortly after the game, Dick made his way through an aisle of gunmetal-gray lockers in the midst of other Central players changing out of their uniforms. He went directly into one of the tiled bathroom stalls, closed the door, threw up in the toilet, and flushed it simultaneously to help drown out the retching sound. *I really don't want to get the flu,* he thought, and he vowed to stay healthy. He didn't have the flu.

The next week, Central fans witnessed a brutal game against Akron Saint Vincent, lasting two and a half hours due to game stoppages for injuries—one of them costing us the services of our star quarterback as a crushing tackle broke Dick's collarbone. Obviously, other coaches were teaching their players to tackle correctly as well. Dick was slammed to the ground, his helmet hitting hard with impact.

Dick tried to stay in the game, but Coach McVay took him out. Dick was confused and disoriented. After nothing more than the ritual administration of smelling salts, the team doctor attended to the obvious injury of the collarbone. Dick would not return until the final two games of the season, including our only loss of the year to Youngstown East.

Stark County loves their high school football players and athletes. With his senior year coming to a close, he was awarded All-County and All-City honors as quarterback, despite playing only four games. In all, he received twelve varsity letters in the three major sports in his four-year high school career—a first in Ohio.

* * *

Just as Dick had predicted to Jane earlier, the college offers started to roll in. I don't think there was a school of national importance that didn't want Dick on their football roster. I remember the big box of offer letters on his desk in the bedroom, separated between football and baseball. He was proud of the offers from Ivy League, Big Ten, and West Coast schools, telling me some offers were for academic performance as well. That made a big impression on me.

After numerous offers, particularly from Big Ten teams, Dick accepted a full athletic scholarship for football in 1960 from Michigan State University in East Lansing. The beautiful campus and the leadership of Duffy Daugherty as the head football coach were too much to resist.

Prior to 1962, the NCAA required head coaches to

recruit in public settings, typically at the player's high school or a restaurant. So when the NCAA allowed coaches to recruit inside the home of prospective players, Coach Daugherty must have thought it was a license to steal. He was a master recruiter with exceptional relationship skills. Parents loved him. Duffy understood the concept of a student-athlete and treated the parents and players with respect.

It was nothing like the scenario we experienced in Columbus at Ohio State. Woody Hayes waved to us from the athletic field house parking lot as we left. My parents were in the front seat, my dad driving, with Dick and me in the backseat. Things became quiet as we pulled away.

Finally, my mom broke the silence and said, "I don't like that man." This was from the nicest person living in the state of Ohio, who never had a bad thing to say about anyone.

No explanation was needed. It was obvious to all that Woody was the antithesis of the student-athlete concept preached by my parents.

That same year, older brother John put in his transfer from Ohio State to MSU because of the university's excellent forestry program. *Not sure how that will work between the two of them, considering their history of sibling rivalry,* I thought. *We'll see.*

Along with everyone else, I was proud of Dick. I knew firsthand how good he was and what he had accomplished. Despite his goal-driven persona, he always treated me as an equal on and off the field.

Ken Bankey and Dick, both quarterbacks, recruited John Walsh, a center from Chicago's Brother Rice High School, as their third roommate in the Brody group of dorms right across from the Kellogg Center, the on-campus hotel. John remembers his own immaturity as a freshman and how Dick led as a role model in campus behavior. At that time, "I was all giggles," John told me. Ken also recalled how those early college days were developmentally important, with Dick's role modeling, focus, and leadership about studies and general responsibilities. Both John and Ken remembered that Dick just seemed to be smarter than everyone else—or at least that he carried himself that way. They remained friends throughout college and well into life.

This closeness with teammates and rivals was a new experience for Dick. Maybe it was the higher maturity level in college, or maybe it's because really good athletes find it easier to bond with others of equal skill. Regardless, Dick was at home at Michigan State.

CHAPTER 4

Dick always stuck by me . . .
family lessons learned about brothers.

My transition to being the only kid at home and out from
under the shadow of an All-Everything brother opened many
doors. Not all of them good.

The great facilitator of the good, the bad, and the ugly
was the unconstrained access to our second car, which I no
longer had to share with Dick: a 1954 Ford, stick shift on the
column, Fiesta hubcaps, and whitewall tires. I had it made.
At first, the opportunity was positive as I took responsibility
for the car. "Car days" in the spring with my friends were
the best. The four of us converted the driveway basketball
court into a detail shop. My dad beamed as he saw the clean,
shiny cars and laughed when the day ultimately turned into
a water fight with the hoses.

"We can bring our cars to my house on Saturday," I told
Bruce, Bill, and Tim.

Tim Streb had been my best friend from age two, and
Bill Leahy and Bruce Correll were friends from high school.
My friendship base had expanded exponentially because
Central was the only Catholic high school drawing students

from the greater Canton metropolitan area. There were at least eight public high schools covering the same area. The four of us played football and pretty much thought we were "King Shit."

"What time?" Bill asked, knowing it was always a pain in the ass to pin Streb down to a time.

"Ten works. Everyone has to bring their own car polish, though."

Tim had access to his dad's new Pontiac Bonneville convertible; Bill had his own new VW Beetle convertible; and Bruce had "the Stud," a 1948 Studebaker four-door with running boards. The thought was to wash and polish the cars for our dates that night.

On Sundays, we would have our cars ready for our own version of a car rally. This particular Sunday, we were headed to Mohican State Park, southwest of Canton by about two hours. Beer bottle caps weren't the only thing to come off on these trips, as enough clothes were discarded by the guys and girlfriends to warrant a trip to the confessional the following week.

Taking care of the car on Saturdays, and even washing the primary family car at the same time, went a long way to underpin my credibility. My friends and I had successfully established a belief pattern with our parents that we were normal teenage kids, so liberal access to the cars was within our responsibility. For the most part, we were good kids, but maybe I received the benefit of the doubt thanks to a brother who had demonstrated unusual responsibility by age sixteen.

* * *

CHAPTER 4

That benefit of the doubt paid off handsomely the summer of 1960, between my sophomore and junior years.

"Dad, some of my buddies on the football team and I have an idea that sounds like fun."

"What is it, Jimmy?" Dad said while shifting his attention from helping Mom with the dishes to me.

"Well, it involves camping. Our plan is to be gone until a week from Sunday."

That was when Mom stopped washing the dishes to give full attention to our little talk.

"That's eight days from now." Dad paused, but I could see the gleam in his eye. "What's your plan?" He always had a keen sense of adventure.

I explained that we had picked out Raccoon Creek State Park in West Virginia, about 120 miles away, close to Pittsburgh.

"We'll have to keep our food in the ice chest and do our own cooking on the Coleman stove. We're hoping the hiking is really good," I added, emphasizing the wholesome aspects of our plans.

"Who's going to drive?"

"Well, that's why Bill, Bruce, and I need your permission to use our car." At that time, our '54 Ford was the only car that made sense to use.

"None of you have turned sixteen yet. You need a driver with a permanent license."

It was time to play my ace in the hole. "Larry Wish is sixteen. He's going too." Larry happened to be the one kid every parent trusted—what a great cover.

"I don't think this is a very good idea, Len," my mother interrupted with an authoritative tone. She dried her hands on her apron, although it looked more threatening with a

45

series of twists whenever she was stressed.

Dad paused, looked at Mom, then looked me straight in the eye, paused again, and turned back to Mom. "These boys have to grow up sometime."

Three fifteen-year-olds and one sixteen-year-old were off on a weeklong adventure. We managed to get our camp-site set up and meet some girls the very same day at the "swimmin' hole"—this was West Virginia, after all. As luck would have it, there were four of them, the oldest being eighteen, who had the job of chaperoning the three younger ones—all about fifteen. Life was good as our education in the finer elements of the female persuasion continued. Thank God for Larry Wish.

* * *

In one fashion or another, date night almost always involved Tim and me and Marcia and Toni, our girlfriends. When I was driving the Ford on a date, I liked the reflection of the clean car in the big retail shop windows as we drove by, especially the way the Fiesta hubcaps captured the afternoon light as they turned. Our activities always led to making out whenever possible. With four in the car, things were pretty tame. In time, we learned that dropping the other couple off early always led to more excitement. None of us really knew what we were doing, and I'm surprised no one ended up pregnant. The trips to the confessional with a priest who knew every boy's voice by heart was an overwhelming act of humiliation and embarrassment.

With Saturday being date night, we somehow got this idea that Friday would be fight night. We thought we were pretty tough. Just the word *rumble* brought out the worst in each of us. Tim was almost always the instigator.

"I've got an idea for tonight with those assholes in town," he said late one Friday afternoon.

Central was one of the smallest high schools in Canton, which must have contributed to a bit of a Napoleon complex on our part.

Stupid really was the operative word for much of what we did on Friday nights, as the street fights were sometimes preceded by drinking and shoplifting cigarettes. I don't think any of us were proud of our actions.

Sometimes we weren't that lucky, and circumstances didn't always end that well, as the case when six of us ended up in the Massillon holding cell for disorderly conduct. Fortunately, Bruce wasn't with us that night. His dad, Judge Correll from Canton, ultimately influenced his Massillon counterpart to give us a lenient outcome.

Upon seeing me behind bars, my dad's only comment was, "You look good there! You've embarrassed the family name." He turned around and left me to my own defenses, as he wasn't about to put up with the line of BS he knew I was about to serve up. What I interpreted was, *We never had to put up with this from your brothers, especially Dick.*

I was finding my own way, but not necessarily a good one as I struggled. I knew I had taken a serious departure from the standards Dick had set. While I didn't get caught very often, my behavior in general was enough to disappoint my parents a great deal that summer. Maybe I knew I couldn't compete with Dick for positive attention, so I subconsciously chose this direction for any attention at all.

* * *

Yet Dick always stuck by me. Maybe it was because my grades were good and my athletics were strong, or maybe it was just a big brother looking out for a little brother. The lessons my parents had taught Dick about brothers were well learned, at least where he and I were concerned. He continuously had my back as we grew up. He really came through for me one night in particular when our parents were out of town.

A new friend, Dave Rentschler, joined our group the summer of 1961 and expanded our imagination with access to the "Melrose Missile," a drab-green '49 Plymouth four-door he could "borrow" from his neighbor on a regular basis. Streb coined the name after a top drag racing machine of the time. It was kind of a piece of junk. Sneaking a parent's car—or neighbor's car, in this case—out of a garage in the middle of the night gave us the excitement necessary to feed our imagination. Dave—or "George," as most of us called him—would secure the "Missile" and pick up each of us after our parents were asleep, and then we'd be off for a night's worth of adventure.

"Goddamn, I think we're out of gas!" George exclaimed from the driver's seat of the old Plymouth.

"Shit, I'm screwed," Streb said.

We learned over the years that Tim didn't always handle pressure well, and that night was no different. It was 4:00 a.m., and we were on Jackson Avenue, about twelve miles from home. His parents would be getting up around six, and this little event would be the last straw in a long line of misfortune that summer. I was lucky; my parents were on vacation. With Dick home from college, he was left in charge of the house—and, unfortunately for him, of me too.

"What are we going to do?" George was concerned, as it was certain he would get caught for stealing the car.

"Isn't there a phone booth at the gas station on the corner of Jackson and Tusc?" I asked.

No one was sure. This was a quiet section of Jackson Avenue—absolutely no traffic.

"Here's what I'll do. I'll run to the station and call Dick. We have a five-gallon can of gas in the garage for the lawn mower. Maybe he'll bring it to us."

"Won't he tell my dad?" Tim said.

"I don't think so. I'll make something up. He doesn't need to know the details. At least it's a plan."

My contribution to our group always seemed to be talking our way out of trouble.

It took about ten minutes to jog the mile to the station, where the phone booth was as I remembered. Dick answered as if still wide awake—odd, but I didn't go into it.

"I'll explain later, but we need your help. We're out of gas on Jackson Avenue, and Dave and Tim will be in big trouble if their parents find out they've been out all night."

"I thought you were in bed. What am I supposed to do?" Dick asked with a clear tone of exasperation.

I explained the plan, and he agreed. Once the car had gas, I rode home with Dick. After dropping Tim off, George returned the car at 5:30 a.m. and slipped into his house unnoticed—just under the wire. George's mother could never understand why teenage boys needed so much sleep—it was generally noon before he'd get up.

"Do I need to know what happened last night?" Dick said the next day. "Mom and Dad left me in charge, and we have another week to go before they're back from Minnesota. I'd rather not have to explain a lot of trouble."

"You won't," I said. "Thanks for bailing us out. By the way, what was with you last night? You were wide awake when I called. You mentioned a few things on the way home, but it didn't seem like the time to talk. What's up?"

"I don't want this to go anywhere until Mom and Dad know, but Diane and I are pretty serious. We talked about getting married, but we're not sure it's the right decision until I get my degree."

Dick trusted my ability to keep a secret—probably because he had so many things on me, he could hang my ass out to dry anytime he wanted. Still, it made me feel important that he confided in me about their plans.

"Wow! That is news. What will her parents think?"

"They're good people, and she's an only child, so they want the best for her. My feelings are that they would jump for joy if I proposed."

In many respects, Diane was a terrific match for Dick. The only stumbling block was her occasional self-focus, the result of being an only child. When it kicked in, the competition for praise and adulation with Dick was on. I overheard my parents talk about it a few times. Dick and Diane were definitely both performers and needed a stage. Was there enough room in their relationship for both egos to survive?

* * *

Events started to settle down that fall. Dick was back at MSU, and I survived the summer, despite many opportunities for tarnishing the family name. Getting back under the wing of Coach McVay for our senior year of football was a good thing. We continued to learn how to take responsibility for ourselves under adverse conditions. With a number of future Division I–bound athletes on our team—Becherer, Blubaugh, Melchior, Palumbo, Page, and myself—we were solid. I can assure you that practices were harder than ever, as McVay and the coaching staff knew they had the horses for a great year. As it turned out, a 10–1 season was pretty good, but we knew we blew the one loss to Akron Saint Vincent's.

Looking back, the highlight for me was during fall practice, before the season even began.

"I've got a little treat for you men today," Coach McVay said after gathering the team together before calisthenics at practice. "We've got a tough schedule ahead of us, and I want to make sure we're ready for our first game in two weeks, so I've arranged for a little scrimmage today. After you're on the bus, I'll let you know who we're playing."

He had never done this before, and excitement was sky-high.

When we turned left onto Tuscarawas Avenue, I knew immediately we were headed to Massillon. The Tigers had never scheduled the Central Catholic Crusaders on their regular season schedule—rumor was that our team might be too good.

"Men, the coaches and I have set up a little round robin scrimmage with three other pretty good teams—Massillon, Marion Harding, and Toledo Central Catholic."

The bus exploded with a unified cheer that was pure joy. Because I grew up in Massillon, I was especially psyched. We always lived with being second best in Stark County, and while this contest was only a scrimmage, it was as close as we would come to marquee status. Scrimmages are set up so teams can improve; the outcome of a "winner" isn't in the cards. It was safe to say, though, that the four teams on the field that day represented the top echelon of high school football in the state of Ohio that year. Local reporters who saw our scrimmage speculated there was another "big dog" in town in 1961—the Central Catholic Crusaders.

I thought of Dick a few times during the game. He had definitely helped define the winning, hard-nosed football culture we had developed under Coach McVay. This opportunity was big, but Dick missed out. Had the scrimmage happened two years earlier, it would have been a chance for the two best quarterbacks in the state to face off—Dick and Joe Sparma. Later in life, both would be inducted into the Stark County High School Football Hall of Fame on the same day.

Months later, we seniors were honored at the annual football award banquet, with Michigan State head coach Duffy Daugherty and defensive coach Hank Bullough as guest speakers. Hank Bullough had been a coach at Canton Timken before taking his position at State. The men's booster club prepared their best rigatoni with Italian sausage to everyone's delight, as we were served on the basketball court prior to the ceremony. To this day, rigatoni is my favorite Italian pasta. Each time I had it, I received an award—what's not to like?

I had met Duffy before through Dick, but I had not seen him in front of an audience.

"When I'm looking for great linemen, like Dave Behrman from Dowagiac, Michigan," he explained to the audience, "I generally do it in rural communities. I look for young men plowing the fields on the family farm. I stop and ask for directions to the nearest town." He pauses. "And if the young man picks up the plow with one arm and uses it to point the direction, I give him a scholarship right then and there . . . before Michigan finds out where he lives."

Parents roared with laughter.

"On the other hand, some people have been pretty complimentary of my coaching. Take Canton's own George Saimes, for example. He came to us with four-four forty speed; powerful, all-around athletic skills in three sports; and a quick mind. But he probably wouldn't have amounted to much if it wasn't for my coaching."

People laughed again. Duffy was on a roll.

"The coaching staff thinks he has a great shot at All-American again this year."

The audience erupted with applause. George was well liked and respected as a great player from Canton Lincoln, and many of us took pride in playing against him.

"Maybe one of yours, like Dick Proebstle, will follow him."

A standing ovation.

Regardless of the future of Central's football program, Dick's legacy would always remain—an influential leader molded as a quintessential high school quarterback under Coach McVay's guidance.

CHAPTER 5

"He took a beating on that play."
Dick was disqualified from play for the
remainder of the season.

Duffy wasn't just recruiting players at Central. Coach McVay also joined Michigan State in the fall of 1962 as a member of the coaching staff, with Dick and me as full-scholarship athletes. With brother John also at MSU, it was a trifecta for my parents. Two boys on full scholarship with two coaches they trusted, and all three boys in the same place—at least until John graduated.

Surprisingly, my confidence from high school success took a nose dive as a freshman on the football team. Maybe I wasn't as prepared as I thought. Maybe it was MSU's seventy-six-thousand-capacity stadium. Maybe the "little brother" expectations. Regardless, what once came easy left me—left me holding nothing but my jock. I was missing blocks and dropping passes. Not a sustainable formula for building a solid reputation with the coaches. Plus, I had developed an attitude over time. I can say that being constantly called "Dick" didn't help. It was as if I didn't exist. Luckily, my classroom performance kept me off the "concerned list" scrutinized by freshman coach Burt Smith.

Dick prodded to keep me on track, but I was a work in progress. He never gave up on me.

"You're going to have to put more into it. This isn't high school," he told me.

As a backup quarterback, Dick held the players' respect with his attitude, work ethic, and performance on and off the field. He was now surrounded by players at his level— or higher—and he felt more a part of the team than in high school. He genuinely wanted me to experience the same thing, but he wasn't going to mother-hen me.

* * *

On September 12, 1962, Dick was working exceptionally hard to earn the starting quarterback position. He was determined as ever to excel as he ran the first-string offense that day in a full-contact team scrimmage.

We freshmen were practicing separately on a different field, so I never got a clear description about what happened, other than "he got hammered" while in a classic upright pocket-passing pose. Quarterbacks didn't wear red shirts for protection in those days. Apparently, two defensive linemen hit him simultaneously from both sides.

Practice was moved to another part of the field as Dick was tended to. The trainers brought him in a pickup truck to Olin Health Center on campus, and he was admitted within fifteen minutes. The surreal sight of the truck leaving the field was reminiscent of a gladiator being removed from the Colosseum in ancient Rome. Every player knows it could have been him.

CHAPTER 5

The medical records state that previously, on September 5, "Dick had been bumped on the left lower chest and sustained a severe contusion to the lower left anterior chest wall and rib area and was incapacitated for five days."

"Bumped" was an odd term, considering it required a five-day recovery. Records from this injury on the twelfth state that "during a scheduled scrimmage session, the subject received a hard block in the area just beneath the left rib cage. He sustained a severe contusion to the spleen and was hospitalized for the next sixteen days."

Chymoral and Seconal were prescribed for "feelings of syncope [fainting] and for sleep," so he was a little out of it when I saw him the next day.

"How are you doing?" I asked after entering the room. My first glance told me he would be here for a few days.

"I'm not sure." Every word coming out of Dick's mouth was accompanied by the pain of breathing, which aggravated his multiple internal injuries.

We talked a little more, but he started to tire quickly.

"I'll call Mom and Dad to let them know you'll be okay. Rest up and get well."

After leaving Dick's room, I saw Doc Furig in his white coat walking down the hall, stethoscope around his neck and clipboard in hand. He was our team doctor and had a pretty good file on most of us.

"What do you think, Doc? Will he be okay?"

"It'll take a while, Jim."

Doc was a big man with a kindly face—cherubic. He was always open to letting us know what he thought, with an added dose of good advice.

"I didn't see what happened, but the coaches told me he took a beating on that play. The injuries will heal, but it will take some time. He's bright, with a good future. He needs to rest up."

Dick was discharged from the hospital on September 15, only to experience an "inability to sleep in the dorm." Sensitivity to light and noise, combined with sleep disturbance, represents classic post-concussion symptoms, yet a concussion was never diagnosed. On September 18, he was readmitted to Olin and finally discharged again on September 28. No medical notes were added to his record during that ten-day period.

Despite Dick's attempt to return to active participation, the injury remained symptomatic. Duffy must have agreed with Doc Furig's medical recommendation and assessment of Dick's potential. He offered Dick the opportunity to red-shirt that season so the Big Ten could grant him another season of eligibility. He was physically disqualified on October 13, 1962, for the remainder of the season. Dick's only game action involved two punts against North Carolina in the season opener.

* * *

My maturation and development in college continued at a snail's pace. I started making more trips home that winter to see Toni, my high school sweetheart. Home was a comfort zone, as I hadn't settled into college life yet. And even the journeys themselves opened new doors with more opportunities to grow up.

"No, you can't borrow my car to go home," Dick said clearly to one of my requests.

He would let me use it for important dates on campus,

but I think he knew going home was a trap that would keep me from finding my way.

Dick thought denying my request would keep me from making the 240-mile trip. So did I, for that matter. What neither of us counted on was my growing attraction to hitchhiking. I began to look at hitchhiking as an adventure, many times leaving at 10:00 on a Friday night, only to arrive around 3:00 or 4:00 in the morning. As I look back, the trips seem to be a metaphor for me finding my own way, something that came to Dick so easily.

One night at about 11:30, while making my way through the streets of Toledo, a two-door '52 Pontiac stopped, and the driver offered me a ride. I had a duffel of dirty clothes for Mom that I could hold on my lap, but the car already held three adults in the backseat, a man and a German shepherd on the front bench seat, plus the driver.

"I'll wait for someone else," I said. "Thanks for stopping."

"You won't take up that much room," the driver said. "Besides, I'm dropping them off," he said, gesturing to the others, "in about a mile. I'll take you out to the interstate, where it'll be easier to get a ride. Besides, it's cold, pal."

He did make sense, as this stretch was proving difficult to find a ride. Even though the situation looked out of control, he got out of the car, put my duffel inside the doghouse sticking out of the trunk, and opened the passenger door.

"You'll fit."

At six-five, 225 pounds, and reasonably experienced via my many "fight nights" in high school, I wasn't too concerned, but I sure as hell was amused. There we were, six adults and a full-grown German shepherd packed in the car, happy as larks, making our way through Toledo at midnight.

"How far did you say we have to go?" I asked, confirming my understanding of the situation.

"Not far," the driver responded.

True to his word, we rounded the corner in an urban neighborhood, with our destination less than one hundred feet away, when suddenly the engine fan belt snapped. We coasted to a stop right in front of their house as if the mishap was planned, and for the next hour, we worked at replacing the fan belt. By the time I reached the interstate, it was almost 1:30 a.m.

We shook hands as friends, and the driver said, "I'm glad we met. Good luck on getting a ride."

It was hard to imagine that people could be this generous.

With barely enough time to get situated with my thumb out and in a good spot under a light, a truck driver headed to Akron picked me up, which was perfect, because Akron was thirty miles north of my home. I slept most of the trip and woke just as we entered a downtown intersection I recognized.

"This is where I'll drop you off," he said. It was probably only the third or fourth sentence of communication the whole trip. "It's late, but there's generally traffic most of the time," he added as I exited the cab.

"Thanks. I appreciate the lift."

He was right, as it wasn't a short time before a man in his thirties stopped and offered me a ride. There was no question he'd been drinking and was a little worse for wear, but I wasn't in a position to be picky.

"Where're you headed?" he said with a definite slur.

"North Canton."

"Right on my way. Hop in."

The car reeked of booze, but another odor also prevailed—kind of an iron scent. Something I'd smelled before, but I couldn't place it. I quickly realized I would need to keep a close eye on his driving. I chose the tactic of conversation to keep his attention.

"What are you doing out so late?" I asked.

The conversation would help me as much as it would help him. Driving in the winter at that time of night always created a feeling of detachment—the repetitive streetlights clipping by with a crystalline reflection from the snow and ice framed against the pitch-black backdrop as we passed. It always seemed surreal to me that I was placed in that exact point in time—like a visiting time traveler.

"I had a run of bad luck at the last bar. Got in a fight over a pool game and took a knife in the side. I'm a little light-headed. That's why I picked you up . . . to make sure I'll be okay."

"Show me," I said. "By the way, what's your name?"

"Chuck Barton," he replied. He turned on the interior light and showed me a six-inch bloodstain on his right side above the hip—the iron smell. "I think it'll be okay if it just stops bleeding."

"You need a hospital, Chuck."

"Can't do that," he said. "My parole officer isn't very forgiving."

"Are you okay to drive, or would it be better if I drove?"

"Driving gives me something to do. Just tell me where you want to go, and I'll take you there."

At 4:30 a.m., we pulled into my family's driveway at Lake Cable in North Canton. "Turn off the engine, and come on in. We can get a better look at that wound inside."

I wasn't sure how my parents would react, but I knew it was the right thing to do. Besides, with three boys, Mom was very experienced in patching up wounds. Hopefully she could do this one too, as I sure didn't want Chuck to get into more trouble. Maybe he did have an ulterior motive in picking me up, but to go out of his way and take me to my front door was pretty righteous.

There we were—Mom, Dad, myself, and Chuck in the kitchen, with Chuck sitting in the very position I remembered Dick in while getting a dressing down a few years previously. Coffee was made, and Mom went to work. With his shirt pulled up, she cleaned the wound and applied a painful application of Mercurochrome. It was a relatively small puncture. Dad put in three butterfly stitches to hold it closed. It didn't look too bad. I made him a sandwich, and after the coffee, he was on his way by 6:00 a.m.—wouldn't consider staying any longer. He did accept the thirty dollars my dad gave him. His money had been taken in the bar scuffle as well.

I thought about that night for a while—just some of the strange experiences while hitchhiking home. They were a wake-up call for me to start growing up and taking responsibility. Reflecting on how these three particular strangers went out of their way to help me that night reminded me of the way Dick was always willing to help me. His standards were high, and as it turned out, I was a slow learner. But nonetheless, his influence had substantial effect. As he told someone at IBM later, "Jim's a winner. Hire him." In a convoluted way, the opportunity to be in Dick's shadow taught me to be a winner.

CHAPTER 5

* * *

As Dick's college experience continued, his relationship with Diane deepened. Their commitment to a chaste relationship lasted over three years, probably leading to their motivation to get married before his graduation at Michigan State. He was twenty-one and she was twenty, a tough age to stay on track sexuality-wise—especially when I consider that my sex education was a self-guided journey with little parental input. I can only assume Dick's education may have been even more restricted with his diligent acceptance of our Catholic education. As a result, Dick and Diane planned their wedding day for August 24, 1963, at Sacred Heart Church in Canton. They would have barely enough time to get established in married housing at MSU before fall practice began.

Dick and I talked a lot about sports but not about such things as the affairs of the heart. A few weeks prior to the wedding, my curiosity couldn't stand any more stoicism.

"When did you ask her?"

"Not too long ago . . . in June."

"What was it like? I mean, what are the details?"

"Not too much to tell."

"What do you mean, not too much to tell? How many times do you ask a girl to get married?"

"Okay . . . okay. We went to dinner at Bender's. You know, the place we had dinner when we double-dated for the homecoming dance a few years ago. It's in that square brick building around the corner from the courthouse. You should know where that is," he jabbed.

"Easy, big brother," I replied, laughing. "What did you eat . . . when did you ask her . . . You know, the important stuff?"

"I had a steak, and Diane had shrimp, and we got so involved with the great food, our conversation, and the old-fashioned wood paneling atmosphere that I almost forgot why I was there. It was really nice. We were talking a lot when Mr. and Mrs. Hadden stopped by our table, and I totally lost track of the ring I had in my pocket."

Mr. and Mrs. Hadden were friends of my parents. They simply had nothing but good things to say about Dick and me and were always at our games.

"What did you do?"

"You know my favorite food is ice cream, so I decided to go to Taggarts for dessert. I could ask her there. I had a double ice cream, and she had the Bittner—you know, their specialty."

"I hope your marriage lasts as long as it takes for you to get to the point. Did she say yes right away? Did you propose on your knee? Where there other people around? C'mon—what gives?"

"It turned out perfect. The place isn't very big—you know, just a few casual tables. We had a table in the corner. I guess there were other people there, but I didn't notice. It felt like we were alone. So I took the ring out, opened the box, got on one knee, and said, 'Will you marry me?' Others must have been watching, because they started to applaud when she said yes. She was so happy, she cried. Made me cry a little too."

"You two deserve each other. I'm happy for you both. But you're cutting things close with fall practice. What did the coaches say?"

"They were great . . . promised to have a place reserved for us at Spartan Village in married housing. Duffy gave me a personal call of congratulations. Makes me look forward to getting back to school. But Diane's a little nervous, I think. She's giving up an opportunity at the University of Cincinnati College-Conservatory of Music for her voice."

"Why would she do that? She really does have talent."

"Her mom instructed her that being with me at MSU would be the better choice. She's old school. I can only guess that she thinks my potential success will bring more stability. You gotta remember that Diane's parents never really made it out of the steel mill mentality."

"Doesn't MSU have a school of music?" I responded.

"Probably. We'll look into it when we get there," Dick said with a shrug.

* * *

With Dick returning to campus married the fall of 1963, he renewed his focus on the goal of securing the starting quarterback position. Fall practice picked up right where spring practice had left off—it was intense.

In the spring, Dick and Steve Juday, a growing friend of mine from our freshman class, had competed hard for the position. Dick tried his best to make up for a lost season and injury. Steve remembers the twenty days of spring practice as "the most competitive of [his] career." In the Green-White Spring Game, Dick and Steve were co-winners of the Best Offensive Back award. Their intense competition resumed in the fall, with each player trying his hardest to win the starting position.

The day before the '63 season opener against North Carolina, Duffy called both players to his office and made the private announcement that Steve would lead the team. No reason was given, although Dick's perfectionist approach sometimes got in the way of his ability to improvise under pressure. Steve still admits his surprise and remembers how professionally Dick handled the disappointing news. Dick remained an inspiration for Steve, as he continued to work hard and challenge Steve in practices, ready to take the position back if Steve let up.

Before we knew it, we were at midseason. Dick's injuries continued, getting his "bell rung" on a few more occasions. His performance suffered a little, but he never gave up.

People always talked about Dick's ability to roll out right and throw a pass with his right hand and, alternately, roll out left and throw with his left hand. That skill alone caused several quarterbacks to look for new positions. This was a definite strength. In reviewing game films years later, however, I noticed that Dick had become reluctant to make the necessary block on the defensive end or corner-back when he led a student body sweep—to make contact by leading with the head and then slide to the shoulder to pin the defender. The quarterback was a primary blocker on those plays and critical in stopping defensive penetration. What was once a strength was becoming a shortfall in his overall quarterback duties.

In the sixth game of the season against Wisconsin, Steve suffered a shoulder injury on a similar student body sweep. It provided Dick with his first opportunity as the starting quarterback. He finished the game with a 30–13 win over the Badgers, followed the next week with a 23–0 win against Purdue, and a 12–7 win over Notre Dame on November 16. The Spartans were ranked No. 4 in both polls.

CHAPTER 5

The last game at home against No. 8 Illinois was scheduled for November 23, but it was delayed one week due to the assassination of President Kennedy. It was a dramatic time for everyone. On that Friday, Duffy gathered the team, and with tears in his eyes, he told us what happened in Dallas. The game was to be played the Saturday following Thanksgiving. What would turn out to be Dick's last start ended in a disappointing 13–0 loss. With the lack of offensive output, our Rose Bowl chances went up in smoke.

Regardless of the season-ending letdown, Dick and I did manage to make the 1963 team highlight film together on one play against Wisconsin. I came in as a sub late in the game. It was supposed to be a roll out pass right, with me running an out pattern. I was wide open, but Dick chose to run. My peel-back block put the defensive player out of the game and into the cheap seats. The crowd roared, and Dick scored one of his two touchdowns that year—brother helping brother.

What hurt was Dick's lack of confidence in me catching the ball—probably a wise decision on his part and a reality check for me. Even my own brother had lost confidence in my pass-catching ability. In truth, I was still distracted and not giving 100 percent as I continued to explore the many freedoms offered an underclassman away from home.

Two months later, in January of '64, Dick made three trips back to Olin Health Center for "tension syndrome and nausea." That's when the migraines started. How exactly a migraine works isn't known, and it can be different for each person. At that time, the medical connection for migraines was thought to be anxiety, not traumatic brain injury from concussions.

* * *

The following year, Dick and Diane became proud parents. Michael James Proebstle was born at Sparrow Hospital in Lansing, Michigan, on August 29, 1964. He was baptized shortly thereafter at the Saint John Student Parish, a Newman Center serving the MSU campus Catholics.

Everyone was healthy, and Dick and Diane were thrilled—naturally. Michael was the firstborn grandchild in our immediate Proebstle family, edging out John's firstborn son, Mark Andrew Proebstle, by a shade more than three months—things never change.

As James Michael Proebstle, I was honored to be Michael's godfather. We were all growing up, beginning to take our place in adult society. But fall practice was right around the corner, and for Dick, the new roles of husband and father added to the existing pressure of only being a backup quarterback.

* * *

During a morning full-contact scrimmage in September 1964, before the opening North Carolina game, Dick and I were playing together on the second-string offense. Dick was determined as ever to excel as he ran the offense that day against the first-string defense. When he called the look-in pass with me as the primary target, he made eye contact in the huddle, as if to say, *Make it good.*

I'll always be relieved I caught the pass—it was the last one he ever threw to me. In my eye, I saw a perfect spiral. It was quick and complete, with an immediate tackle. But what

I saw in the background of the catch spelled disaster. Just after his release—once again, in a classic upright pocket-passing pose—three of our biggest defensive linemen hit Dick simultaneously from all sides, the better part of a thousand pounds of testosterone in a reckless-abandon collision. He didn't move, and we all knew it was over. It was like déjà vu, with the scrimmage being moved to another part of the field as Dick was tended to. In a short while, he was admitted to the Olin Health Center.

The medical report states, "He was hit hard on the right side of his headgear during a scrimmage session. He was 'falled' by the impact and momentarily unconscious. His confusion disappeared after approximately fifteen minutes and a generalized headache started to appear. No nausea, vomiting or vertigo." The medical record also simply states that he had received "a moderate to severe cerebral concussion and a moderate to severe contusion to the right temporal-parietal area. The patient had no complaints. No neurological findings. To discharge and follow up as an out-patient."

Looking back, it's interesting that the records show no other treatment, as they normally would for a sprain, broken bone, dislocation, or whatever. Just the word "discharged." The full impact of the concussion was not visible. There wasn't much to be done. There were no follow-up notes in Dick's records, other than a request for the records by the University of Minnesota Law School in August 1965.

Today's research has ultimately shown that a moderate to severe head injury, such as Dick's, can kick off a neurodegenerative disease that can haunt the person many years after "recovery."

I wasn't able to see Dick until the next morning. He

appeared okay.

"How are you doing?" I asked.

"I got hit by a truck." His emphasis wasn't on humor but on fact.

"I saw what happened, Dick. Do you know what happened?"

"No, not really."

I explained what I saw, and before I finished, he said, "Did you catch the pass?"

"Yes, I did."

He smiled and said, "Good."

I was humbled by his sense of pride in me. In all reality, the pass was so good that it would have taken extra effort on my part not to catch it.

When I saw Doc Furig later, I asked, "Will he be okay?"

"We need to be careful of the concussion, but there's not much we can do . . . this isn't his first."

"How many has he had at State?" I asked.

"This is the first one where we've seen him in the hospital, but who knows how many more on the field," Doc replied. "Do you remember his having any issues during high school?"

"I remember references to three concussions, but I'm not really sure. He was still able to play, though. That's just part of the game, isn't it?"

In truth, all of us were hit so many times in the head in practices and games that it would be impossible to tell how many concussions or subconcussive blows we received.

"Maybe, but with this being an important season . . ." He stopped and rephrased his thought. "If he were my son, I'd suggest he hang it up. He's bright, with a good future."

"Thanks, Doc, but I know he'll be disappointed."

As I walked across the MSU campus, past Beaumont Tower and across the Red Cedar River toward Case Hall, I thought more about Dick. I concluded he would have trouble understanding and accepting Doc's advice—hopefully in time, maybe? Diane would be on board right away, however, as her comments about his headaches were growing, even at this early stage of their marriage.

Once again, Duffy must have agreed with Doc Furig, as Dick never suited up again.

Charlie Migyanka, 1964 team captain, has no recollection of Dick returning to the team, although the records show Dick received a varsity letter. The most frustrating summary to Dick's career is those stats for 1964, his final year: no passing yards, no running yards, no time logged on the field. Hard for a quarterback to accomplish and still win a varsity letter.

* * *

Although Dick could no longer play, Duffy saw Dick's potential as a resource. He assigned him as a personal coach to Jimmy Raye—a freshman quarterback from Fayetteville, North Carolina—at the beginning of Jimmy's freshman practice sessions on Old College Field.

From 1962 to 1964, many talented black athletes from the South—Bubba Smith, George Webster, Charlie "Mad Dog" Thornhill, Gene Washington, James Garrett, Jim Summers, Jess Phillips, and Jimmy Raye, to name a few—responded to Duffy Daugherty's recruiting call during the Jim Crow era of NCAA football, when blacks were barred from playing football in most Southern colleges.

Jimmy was struggling to transition from a throwing-quarterback system in high school to a running offense at MSU with a bootleg series, where the footwork was completely different. Jimmy survived playing the quarterback position with Dick's help—maybe one of Dick's most memorable contributions to the game. Jimmy went on to be one of the first black starting quarterbacks of a national championship team when MSU shared that honor with Notre Dame in 1966. His football career continued for a lifetime in the pros as both a player and a coach.

In the book *Raye of Light* by Tom Shanahan in 2014, Jimmy recalls,

> *Burt Smith saved me by having Dick Proebstle work with me. He made sure Dick kept teaching me the fundamentals of the offense. Dick was an exceptional character guy and a great friend and confidant. . . . He taught me the nuances and technical aspect of learning how to run the belly option and the bootlegs. In high school, we were a dive-football team. You didn't lead anything. There was more post-snap football at Michigan State than pre-snap football for me to learn. For a lot of guys, it's difficult.*

Dick's leadership and contribution to MSU football also continued as president of the Varsity Club, typically a role filled by an alumni athlete. Dick held office with distinction.

* * *

I was still off track, yet Dick was never too busy to help. I clearly remember a discussion that influenced my MSU experience and future. Terry Leonard, an MSU wrestler from Oklahoma, and I had become good friends and still remain so, but we were both frustrated at that stage of our college careers. He had a Corvette, and I had an idea.

"Terry, why don't we take a break from school—you know, and experience life?" I think my remembrances of hitchhiking had created a wanderlust luring my attention away from school.

When he responded with a thumbs-up and a few thoughts about the adventures Route 66 could offer us, we were all but out the door. I thought I'd better call Dick so he could relay my plans to our parents.

"You want me to call Mom and Dad, not you? You're still missing the big picture. First off, you're not a kid anymore. And besides, you don't seem to have the balls to call Mom and Dad yourself. What are you running away from, anyway? They will be very disappointed."

"I can't do anything about that. I just don't feel like anything's working here," I said with less conviction.

"So you're going to quit?" He chose the right word, as we were raised to abhor quitting. "This isn't any different from when you were a sophomore at Central and you didn't have the confidence to play varsity basketball when you clearly could have started. You hung around the JV team because it was comfortable. Get your head out of your jock, and do something about what you don't like. People aren't going to hand you things. Quitting won't help."

I couldn't refute anything he said as I reflected on his advice while we sat in the Case Hall grill. His kick in the ass helped me—and Terry, as both of us stayed. After recommitting myself the summer of my senior year to intense workouts and an attitude adjustment, my confidence came back. That fall, I went on to become the first-string tight end starter for all eleven games for our 1965 national championship team, with academic honors at both the Big Ten and NCAA levels. Terry started as a wrestler for his entire season for MSU's 1965–66 national championship team and is in the National Wrestling Hall of Fame in Stillwater, Oklahoma.

* * *

Regardless of all that happened on and off the field for both Dick and me, and regardless of all the good he had contributed to the team, this chapter in Dick's athletic life—which had always been defined by success—did not end the way he had envisioned. In fact, I think it motivated him to overcompensate the rest of his life.

At this point, he was determined to open a new chapter by going to law school at the University of Minnesota.

CHAPTER 6

The migraines were back with an
intensity Dick had never experienced.

"Do you think we'll like living in Minnesota?" Diane said excitedly as they traveled west across Wisconsin on US Highway 14. "I've never been there. I've never been anywhere, for that matter," she said while laughing at her lack of worldliness.

Their son, Mike, was a toddler in the car seat in the back, with boxes and household items packed all around him. They towed a U-Haul trailer behind their 1958 Oldsmobile to move the skimpy amount of furniture from their Spartan Village apartment.

"We have relatives all over the Twin Cities . . . you'll love 'em," Dick replied. "You met a few at the wedding—Aunt Lucille and Uncle Joe, for sure. As far as Minnesota, what's not to like? Excellent lakes and fishing, beautiful outdoors, and the Twin Cities are pretty sophisticated. They'll love your voice. The winters can be tough, but nothing you can't handle."

"Are you sure it's all right to stay at their house until we find an apartment?"

"No problem. Mom and Dad set it up. Everyone looks up to Uncle Joe. His law firm is the biggest in Saint Paul, and it should be a great in when I get my law degree. I expect he'll want to hire me right away."

Our dad and Uncle Joe got their undergraduate degrees together at the University of Minnesota in the early '30s. They earned enough money selling magazines all over the state to pay for room, board, and books. Joe was the sales manager—more like a foreman, as I understood things—as the group of five young men went town to town knocking on doors. Joe married Lucille and became an attorney, while Dad became an aeronautical engineer and fell in love with Lucille's sister, Helen. Their friendship was chiseled into their DNA throughout adulthood.

As an extremely successful attorney, Joe was bigger than life with his five-foot-three-inch frame and bulldog expression, always with a half-smoked cigar or cigarette rounding out his image.

A few years later, in 1968, I would encounter Uncle Joe after receiving my MBA from Michigan State. It seemed as if everyone had to pass inspection with Uncle Joe. I sat down with him in their beautiful art deco home in old Saint Paul—alleyways and garages in the back, homes facing the main boulevard.

"So," he said, sitting in his chair without a smile or an ounce of humor on his face, "your dad says you got an MBA."

Here I was, a six-foot-four, 230-pound starting tight end for MSU's 1965 national championship team, terrified from the intimidation of Uncle Joe's success, trying to muster up the right words to make a good impression.

"That's right, Uncle Joe," I replied respectfully.

"What do you plan to do with your MBA?" The question felt like a hole being bored into my brain.

"I plan to be a consultant," I said.

"And just what is it that you're going to consult at?"

His logic went right to the core of my inexperience and naïveté in thinking the degree would somehow make me an expert at my field of study. I found myself mumbling a reply, something to the effect of, "Good question. I'm still working on that."

To say that Dick was equally impressed with Uncle Joe was an understatement, as Dick was entering Uncle Joe's domain of the law. Dick knew the right steps at the University of Minnesota Law School would lay a bedrock foundation in the profession.

"First things first, though," Dick said to Diane. "We need to find an apartment. We'll pick up a Sunday *Star Tribune* tomorrow and check out the ads. We don't want to wear out our welcome at Joe and Lucille's."

Dick jumped at an opportunity to get a two-bedroom apartment in the northern suburbs in exchange for managing the building. The only cash coming in would be from Diane's singing, and that wouldn't be much or very consistent.

Soon after moving in, they made friends with two other MSU grads at a party for first-year law students: Jamie Blanchard, future governor of Michigan, and Terry Glarner. Terry was from the Twin Cities, and his girlfriend, Val, was from South Chicago. The three men hit it off as they dove into the responsibility of law school. It was an incredible grind designed to flush out 50 percent of the first-year students. Diane became tight friends with Val, and their relationship continued until after her marriage to Terry.

* * *

Midway through his first year, Dick was feeling tremendous pressure. There was no test or guidance to determine where you stood—just one exam at the end of the year. The final grading was based on a system of twenty points. If you scored better than an eight, you moved on to the second year. Eight or less, gone. It created a natural, worrisome pressure.

It was quite a balancing act for Dick to stay on top of his studies, be a husband and a father, keep tenants happy, and be a chaperone for Diane in her growing singing career at a fancy cabaret nightclub called Scheik's. Dick felt he had to do everything. The commute from the suburbs to the U's main campus in the city didn't help any either.

Dick hit the wall sometime around April 1967. Diane was giving two-and-a-half-year-old Mike a bath, and the doorbell rang. Dick was in another room studying. The tub had drained, so she left Mike on his own while she quickly answered the door. It was a neighbor, and they talked for just a few minutes when suddenly loud screams came from the bathroom.

"Oh my God, it's Michael!" she said, running toward the growing intensity of the screams. Had he fallen, broken a bone, banged his head? What could it be? *It's only been a few minutes!* she thought as she raced to her son.

The screams elevated to a sound of torture. Dick arrived simultaneously with Diane to witness the calamity. Mike had pulled himself up to the faucets and figured out how to turn on the water—just the hot water.

"Goddamn it, Diane! What are you thinking?"

Dick's verbal chastising continued as he scooped Mike from the tub. Mike's tender baby skin on his feet and legs was scalded. The trip to the hospital was filled with a lecture about responsibility and how disruptions such as this made Dick's final exam preparation impossible.

Luckily, the burns were mild and only first degree, but the doctor did spend time talking to the parents about the possibility there had been for more serious damage.

"I'm so sorry—it was an accident," Diane said, humiliated and crying in the hospital emergency room.

"No, it wasn't," Dick replied sternly. "You were careless. I can't do everything."

You could feel the tension in the air of Dick's mounting responsibilities.

"You don't seem like irresponsible parents to me," the doctor intervened. "Just be more careful."

Dick fumed about the plural reference of "irresponsible parents" privately as they drove home. *It's unfair,* he thought.

* * *

In May, with only five weeks until the exam, pressure continued to mount. Dick was cramming everything he could from the books when the spots and wavy lines started to appear. The migraines were back with an intensity Dick had never experienced: throbbing pain on both sides of his head, extreme sensitivity to light and sound, and vomiting. The blinding pain behind his right eye rendered Dick unable to read, let alone concentrate. He was completely debilitated, even losing his ability to balance while walking. Diane took Dick to Saint Mary's Hospital, where he stayed for two weeks—precious time needed to prepare for the coming exam.

According to the primary medical theory, a migraine relates to the cerebral cortex and brain stem. One of the brain stem's responsibilities is an integrative function for pain-sensitivity control through sensory pathways. Today, we know that treatment for concussions includes resting the brain, with dark rooms and breaks from studying. Overworking and stressing the brain, as Dick had been doing, only intensifies the problems.

"They're from the concussions," Dick said when Terry visited the hospital to see what he could do to help.

"How many did you have?" Terry asked.

"Five that I can remember."

The conclusion seemed obvious to Dick and Diane. But never in all of Dick's future visits to the hospital did the medical professionals connect the migraines to his concussions.

When Dick was discharged, the stress of trying to catch up was overwhelming. Everyone knew that the final grading was based on a system of twenty points: 19–20 = A; 12–18 = B; 8–11 = C; and less than 8 = gone. Terry scored an 8.3. Dick scored a 7.6—he flunked out.

Dick was devastated for weeks. He had never failed at anything. Terry and Val spent hours with Dick and Diane, trying to console him and help him find a way to recover. The only retesting option was to study on your own for a full year and take the test over.

On December 5, 1967, Dick and Diane became parents for the second time with the birth of Patricia Ann Proebstle, a beautiful, healthy girl with red hair that would define her take-charge personality for the years ahead. Terry and Val were godparents.

Time to earn a living, Dick thought.

"The law isn't for everyone, Dick," Uncle Joe said when Dick finally mustered the courage to meet in Joe's study. "There's no loss of face here. You've got a good brain that any company would be lucky to have."

Uncle Joe was right. In just two years, Dick would be back on top, driving a new Cadillac, and full of testosterone as he began building a formidable business career starting with IBM. It seemed as if Dick was invincible once again.

But the feeling of underachievement in football at MSU and a failed law degree attempt at the University of Minnesota took its toll. The dark days of those migraines would never be completely behind him. They represented an angry, debilitating adversary, always striking when stakes were the highest.

SECTION II

CTE REALIZATION—
YOUR BRAIN SHRINKS . . .
LIFE UNRAVELS

CHAPTER 7

*Dick was subjected to a battery of tests
suggesting the possibility of a mental disorder;
schizoid personality disorder was one hypothesis.*

I followed Dick, taking a job with IBM after receiving my MBA. It wasn't long afterward that we both took a career flyer by leaving IBM and joining a small computer services firm—Dick at the Ohio office and me in LA. Our vision of becoming mini Ross Perots never quite got liftoff for either of us. Very quickly, I joined Xerox in California. Dick joined Northwestern Mutual Life Insurance (NML) and moved his family into a split-level ranch in Chesterland, Ohio, in 1970.

Dick's sales responsibility with NML included a keyman insurance product that positioned him with many local business leaders. As he had at IBM, Dick set many sales records—though there were growing reports of atypical pushy, aggressive selling behavior that caused some clients to seek insurance elsewhere.

Through NML, Dick reacquainted himself with John Lance, a former neighbor where we grew up in Massillon. John now owned Mid-States Equipment, a construction equipment dealership. Dick joined the company with the mutual agreement of taking over ownership from John once Dick was ready.

Little did Dick understand that acquiring a closely held business is always tricky, and as it turned out, this one was no different. The negotiation process with John wasn't about to come together anytime soon.

* * *

Dick was his old "big brother" self when we visited Chesterland in November 1974. Diane was excited too, as she was breaking into the entertainment scene in Cleveland with her singing and also doing some modeling.

"Let's get the kids and go tobogganing," Dick offered shortly after we got our bags unpacked. The kids were itchy to go outside.

The early snow over Thanksgiving was a bonus as far as we were concerned. We grew up tobogganing on the 18th hole of the Brookside Country Club golf course in Canton—and loved it. Since Carole and I were living in Southern California, we hadn't tobogganed in a long while and jumped at the chance.

One of the things we liked about visiting Dick and Diane's family was Dick's insistence on fun activities with the kids. Our kids, Jeff and Jennifer, loved it. With them at seven and five, and Mike and Patty at eleven and eight, you couldn't ask for better kids and a better combination. Dick was a great dad at those age levels.

We gathered up a few sleds and a toboggan, and we were off.

"We'll have dinner at five thirty, so don't be late," Diane

CHAPTER 7

said. She and Carole were looking forward to time together without the distractions.

Dick already had a place mapped out, and the afternoon was perfect. With the kids all bundled up and grinning ear to ear, I remember thinking how ideal their family was. The day in the snow fit right into our expectations until Dick and I managed to push the activity level one step too far, causing Jennifer and Patty to crash into a bushy pine tree. This reduced Jennifer to a pile of tears—not uncommon, as she was the youngest.

Carole used to say, "You just don't know when to stop."

But that's what fathers do, I'd think to myself. Out loud, I'd reply, "She'll survive."

By the time we were back in the car with the dog and four kids, everyone was all smiles again—a *Saturday Evening Post* scene with a toboggan and sleds lashed to the top of the car, kids smiling but exhausted, snow continuing to fall, and two dads in the front seat enjoying the sense of a perfect day.

"I wish we could see you guys more often," I said. "Why don't you bring the family to Anaheim next year?"

"Good idea," Dick responded. "Diane and I have talked about a trip west. Is there enough room to stay at your house?"

"Absolutely. You can see our new place. Plus, I think I can set up a tennis and racquetball match you'll find interesting."

"In what way?" Dick asked.

"In a way that you'll lose both games," I said with a lighthearted verbal confidence that did not match reality, as Dick was a far better tennis player than I was.

"That's not going to happen," he replied quickly with

that all-too-familiar look of competitive determination.

As always, our Thanksgiving visit ended with great memories and an early flight on Sunday back to California.

* * *

It was a shock when Diane admitted Dick into Hillcrest Medical in Mayfield Heights, Ohio, roughly five months later on May 5, 1975. It turned out to be a five-day stay. During his intake exam, he described the five concussions received in football, but the rapid heart rate, flutters, and heavy sweating were the reasons listed as the current illness. His headaches were under control at that time, but his anxiety level was well beyond normal, with the nurse describing Dick as a "perfectionist and high-strung." An EKG and EEG were ordered among various procedures—all with unremarkable results. He had some episodes of anxiety and irritableness, not wanting to talk to his family or answer phone calls. In his discharge summary, it was suggested he see a psychiatrist for psychotherapy.

Diane remembers discussions with the attending doctor about it possibly being a nervous breakdown or a mental disorder. Schizoid personality disorder was one hypothesis, which implied the temporary emergence of pathological symptoms. In 1975, testing procedures were still new and rarely produced definitive results. And as Carole interprets the current *Diagnostic and Statistical Manual of Mental Disorders*, the schizoid personality diagnosis never would have applied to Dick.

It was possible the new job at Mid-States was a stressor, especially considering that the acquisition wasn't progressing to expectations.

"It's an all-or-nothing deal," Dick confided to me in a phone call. "It's the reason I started working there, to learn the business and ultimately take it over. But John is now threatening to pull out of the deal. I don't need that crap, but I'm not going to give up either."

At the same time, Dick was negotiating the purchase of their new home in Massillon—a beautiful estate listed on the historic register. Maybe the pending purchase was a stress trigger as well. Thankfully, the house deal closed, and they successfully made the move on the Fourth of July 1975.

* * *

The following year, Dick and Diane made their promised trip to Anaheim to visit. Discussion about his business was on the back burner, and he seemed relaxed and back to his old self. Maybe that was the role we played in their complicated life.

As planned, an afternoon was set aside for one of our historic tennis and racquetball matches. My strategy, which proved to be valid, was that if you played racquetball first, it would totally screw up your tennis game. Seeing as my strength was in racquetball, he fell into my trap.

Regardless of the outcome, the afternoon took us back to being teens—a timeless remembrance when we just played sports for their pure enjoyment. It was good to see Dick shed the responsibilities he carried so fervently and instead enjoy an experience that transported us to a simpler time, when Dick was just my big brother trying to school me. We smiled and laughed about how things had changed.

It would be nice to recapture the honesty of that moment, as I realize now it was one of the last times Dick would still be Dick.

* * *

Ultimately, the acquisition of Mid-States did go through for Dick in 1980. And after successfully managing through the 1981–82 recession, Mid-States was seemingly under control. Dick was on fire, back on top, fueled by a drive to succeed with a winner-take-all attitude in running his business.

Mid-States was located in Canton, the heart of Ohio's industrial, construction, and farming markets. It was positioned to serve everyone—from the Timken Roller Bearing Company, headquartered in Canton, to the large Amish farming community in central Ohio—with its Bobcat skid-steer and forklift products. Multiple attachments led to the Bobcat's versatility—cleaning out barns, moving industrial supplies in plants, and excavating for new construction were just a few of its capabilities.

In many ways, the Bobcat was the perfect product for Dick. To be a truly competent equipment operator, you needed confidence, dexterity, and excellent hand-eye coordination—assets that played right into his old quarterback skills. Dick was renowned for conducting demonstrations to potential Bobcat customers. Sales came rolling in. With his main office in Canton and new offices in Mansfield, Toledo, and Akron, he controlled the northern Ohio market with an exclusive dealer arrangement with Melroe Manufacturing, the home of the Bobcat product.

His income quickly rose to rival the highest-paid executives of publicly traded companies. For the first time in a while, nothing was in his way, and it felt right.

Tim Helline started working at Mid-States in 1981 and stayed there almost twenty years. As the sales manager, Tim evolved into Dick's only sounding board and confidant. Tim learned "what to do and what not to do" in business, and he credits Dick's mentorship as instrumental in his career today.

"Dick was very smart in how to make things happen . . . just the right way of saying things," Tim said.

Yet to Tim, Dick led a secret life, constantly living in the past with MSU and Central—what he'd accomplished and how he was better than everyone else. Tim saw the changes in Dick morph his behavior firsthand.

"It seemed like his world was getting smaller, not bigger," Tim said. "His decision-making capacity seemed to collapse—out of the blue."

Unexplained events emerged overnight. Something was very wrong.

CHAPTER 8

Dick's brain—his world—was literally shrinking.

Right before our eyes, Dick shifted from being a bigger-than-life overachiever to a secretive, judgment-riddled, take-no-prisoners businessman with a dark, angry personality. After so many years, the impact of Dick's concussions were coming back to haunt him.

Personnel relationships at Mid-States began to unravel quickly for Dick. He frequently became confused about project details, to the point where nobody could follow his directions. He simply didn't make any sense. But if the employees called him on it, he would blast them: "Don't you understand? Can't you follow simple instructions?" It got to the point where employees just nodded and did what they had to do.

The situation devolved as the corporate people at Clark and customers such as Timken grew to dislike Dick more and more for his arrogance and lack of cooperation. Dick would "go off" when Tim provided feedback about what people were saying.

"They wouldn't know if I had millions or had nothing,"

Dick said, reinforcing his secretive, reclusive behavior.

The migraines continued. Tim would find Dick sitting in the office after hours with the lights out, just staring. *Guilt, stress, pressure,* Tim thought.

To make matters worse, Dick apparently began a clandestine affair with Cindy, a secretary at Mid-States. Considering Dick's upbringing and personal standards, the inner conflict and guilt must have been overwhelming with this huge departure of moral conduct.

As Tim relates the scenario, Dick went overboard in buying her a Camaro and financing her house. Then Dick showed up at the office one day with a black eye from a fight. It seemed Cindy's boyfriend, an ex-cop, objected to Dick's involvement. Diane would have her own objections later as well.

Though we didn't understand it at the time, these were early evidentiary markers of CTE dementia taking over Dick's persona. These situations—and many others— marked the beginning of his downfall. They represented a complete departure from his values and sense of responsibility to do the right thing. Only with hindsight do we have some sense about how and why.

* * *

In 1957, Dr. Timothy Leary—the same Timothy Leary who became notorious in the '60s for psychedelic drugs and spiritual revelations—had written many books and constructed an interpersonal typology that fit Dick's behavior in the early 1980s:

CHAPTER 8

*In the pathological form of the "competitive-
narcissistic" personality there is a blind selfishness,
a frantic effort to impress, and a boastfulness and
exhibitionism that becomes flagrant and irrational.*

This typology likely includes many sports superstars. In Dick's case, paranoia fueled a desperate self-focus and attempt to hang on to the past. It was all that made sense to him. It appeared to be arrogance. In reality, however, Dick had become insecure, defensive, and removed—he was no longer himself.

Dick's developing CTE likely stimulated this pathology. In psychology, the textbook case of Phineas P. Gage begins to shed light on the path the brain takes after a traumatic brain injury. In 1848, Gage survived an accident in which a large iron rod destroyed much of his brain's left frontal lobe. The effects on his personality and behavior were so dramatic that people said he was "no longer Gage." Concussions can have a similar effect, although it may take twenty years for the ultimate outcome: the destruction of the brain's neurons.

With CTE, the toxic entanglements and buildup of tau protein reshape the physiology of the brain. They destroy brain cells, causing the brain to atrophy and shrink. This diminishes the frontal lobe, where executive functioning occurs, and impairs the amygdala, which has a primary role in processing emotions and memory. The result is devastating, as the slow process of shrinkage strangles the brain's performance.

Dick's social and critical-thinking skills were being reduced to survival mode. We now recognize the impact of CTE on his judgment, or lack thereof, in areas where he previously showed savvy and expertise.

Dick's offices at work and home had always been "sacred vaults," as Mike called it. Piles and piles of paper would be everywhere, yet Dick had the ability to instantly find the right document, like a random-retrieval computer system. But the pathology of CTE gradually destroyed that retrieval ability, and damage to the hippocampus inhibited consolidation of information from short- to long-term memory. He was left with growing piles, undone responsibilities, unmade decisions, and confused obligations—with no framework for seeking help. It must have been terribly frustrating and confusing for him to function.

* * *

Looking back, it wasn't surprising that Dick's son, Mike, struggled in his high school years in the early '80s. Mike saw how his friends' families interacted—how they lived and worked and functioned—and he knew his family's situation was different. Despite an outward appearance as the perfect family, Mike saw big differences, which were not so good most of the time.

In Mike's mind, his dad was a legend, a superstar placed on a pedestal—the trophy case that adorned their home was a fitting metaphor. In reality, though, Dick was an outstanding high school athlete at Central Catholic and a very good backup quarterback at Michigan State. Had Mike grasped this truth earlier, it may have helped.

As it was, Dick carried a demon look in his eye that Mike learned to fear. Accompanying the look was a set of expectations Mike—nor anyone else—could live up to. When Dick's dissatisfaction manifested itself over the simplest imperfection, he would pause, his face would get red, and he would verbally explode. It reinforced Mike's self-image and psychological baggage of never measuring up. As Mike said,

> With the garage being next to my room in the house, I lived in fear of the garage door opener. When I heard that noise, I knew I would be confronted about whatever I did that day that was unacceptable. Dad micromanaged me to no end. Pulling weeds, raking, simple yard jobs were never done to perfection. A lot of times there was an overall feeling that everyone in our house was "walking on eggshells" so as to not bring on Dad's wrath . . . and not just Patty and me—Mom too.
>
> I did a lot of self-reflection, almost a kind of meditation, and spent a lot of time walking in the woods as a way to escape and figure things out. I enjoyed being at other people's houses. It seemed to torque Dad off when I came home and talked about how so-and-so's parents did this and that, how we had fun, that we talked, and so on.
>
> There were times when we could act like kids, have fun in the house, and speak our minds. But more often than not, we were fixtures, like the furniture. I did enjoy it when my folks had parties, where I could interact with adults, speak my mind, and have people be interested in what I thought and what I had to say. But Dad appeared to get

upset when I mingled at parties. At a very early
age, I could talk with adults about topics of the day,
particularly technology. It seemed all he could talk
about was work. Mom told me at one point that
people found Dad to be basically a bore. Little did
we know that his brain—his world—was literally
shrinking.

Mike could only watch it happen. He remembers times in high school when he happened upon his dad just standing there in a room or outside in the garage, looking down, sometimes scratching his head, kind of talking to himself as if he couldn't remember what he was doing, where he was going, or why he was there. These distant looks and blank stares became more frequent. Mike would say, "What's going on, Dad?" Usually, the reply was, "Oh, nothing."

Dick struggled with remembering names and specific chains of events. He would start talking and lose his train of thought. His frustration made things worse. And whenever Mike talked, Dick didn't listen, as if Mike's role in the conversation wasn't relevant. Mike felt absent and unacknowledged—a feeling perfectly summed up in the current-day expression, "Do you *feel* me?"

As a teenager, Mike was left carrying responsibilities Dick neglected as the head of the household. Mike remembers when the downstairs bathroom pipes froze one winter, which a plumber had to fix. He also remembers having to be the one to track down and replace over sixty screens and storm windows, all in different sizes and shapes. Things, Mike assumed, that Dick just missed, couldn't handle, or forgot about. Instead, Dick was falling asleep in his chair every night. Before leaving for the Naval Academy in 1982, Mike thought, *Who will do this for him when I'm not here?*

* * *

I am embarrassed to say that, along with others, I believed Dick was simply a victim of his own ego, full of himself with the excess of money and braggadocio that come with "success." I was ignorant—we were ignorant—to possible causes for his behavior. We had no other framework to guide our thinking. Like others, we began to push him away.

Dick had fallen into an uncontrollable and unrecognized decline of executive functioning and interpersonal behavior that even he himself was completely unaware of. Sadly, from his perspective, everything was normal. He thought he was on top of his game.

CHAPTER 9

"Fire ... fire!"
Patty screamed at the top of her lungs.
Camelot had come to an end.

"I can't do this anymore," Diane said in protest the Sunday morning after Thanksgiving 1982. The relatives had left the house, and she was emptying the dishwasher. "Our marriage is falling apart, and I'm supposed to entertain family as if nothing is happening? I can't do it!"

"Don't be such a crybaby. I have to deal with these kinds of pressures all the time in business. You can't let it get to you ... Don't panic."

Dick's attitude seemed to parallel a tough series of downs in a football game where the offense absolutely had to score. Panic never solved the problem. *Keep cool,* Dick thought. *Letting the other team see you sweat would only provoke their killer instinct.*

"I don't care who it is, but if I had to guess, I'd bet it's that new secretary. I can't even face my friends."

The truth of her inner feelings emerged. Diane was wrung out trying to deal with Dick's outside relationship. She had no idea whether or not this was his first. She wasn't good at detecting deception, but rumors had begun to grow while Dick functioned as if he were invisible and with no thought of backlash. Canton and Massillon were small communities when it came to people taking notice of prominent citizens cavorting with non-spouses.

"You're not lily-white in this scenario either," Dick countered. "Do you think I don't know what's going on when you stay out for hours past the end of your performances?"

Diane's voice had propelled her career in the Cleveland nightclub entertainment scene. Dick often went to performances and "chaperoned" while she sipped drinks with admiring customers. She craved adulation as much as Dick. It was part of her job. But Dick believed that if he weren't there, the conversation would be of a different nature. His paranoia—likely his intense guilt—was building a barrier in the relationship.

And as irrational as it sounds, Dick boiled with jealousy when compliments for Diane's work came nonstop. One night, after two gentlemen offered Diane a larger stage in Cleveland, assuring her of much bigger audiences, he lashed out: "I don't know why you get all the attention when it's me who makes everything happen!" It was odd—almost as if Dick were more upset about not receiving credit for his manager role than about her suspected extramarital relationship with a customer. They were two stars in a family with room for only one.

"Nothing has ever happened, and you know it!" she screamed.

"I don't believe you! I can't trust you anymore," Dick yelled. "And I can't go to every one of your gigs as a bodyguard."

Both continued cleaning up the kitchen without saying

another word. But the banging of cupboard doors and slamming of silverware drawers was answered with a clashing of pots and pans, creating a surrogate language of anger and mutual dissent. Camelot had broken.

"If you can't trust me anymore, then there's no reason for this marriage to continue," Diane finally said in a firm declaration.

Normally conciliatory, she was startled by her own determination. She privately questioned if she were willing to divorce. It was in complete contradiction to their Catholic upbringing.

"We'll see!" Dick marched out of the room, smashing a coffee cup on the floor in frustration.

He knew a divorce would only make him look bad in a hometown community that clearly favored Diane for her delightful personality with friends and acquaintances and her work at Saint Mary's Catholic Church in music liturgy.

This will be war, he thought.

* * *

In the early morning hours of that Monday after Thanksgiving, Patty awoke to the smell of smoke. Her bedroom was almost right above the new Olympic-sized swimming pool installed in a new south wing of the house.

"Fire . . . fire!" Patty screamed at the top of her lungs.

She noticed billows of smoke encroaching outside her door in the hallway. She saw flames from her window overlooking the pool area.

"Dad . . . Mom . . . Dad . . . Mom!" she yelled as loud as she could. "Get up, get out—the house is on fire!"

Mike had already left that morning to return to the academy.

With barely enough time to grab a bathrobe, Patty ran down the hall to her parents' bedroom and heard her mom choking on the smoke inside. The effect on her sensitive vocal cords was quite evident, and she covered her mouth with a towel. Dick rallied behind her in his sweat suit and tennis shoes. He pushed and then literally carried Diane as they fled down the back butler stairwell.

This home was on the historic register for its role in the Underground Railroad for slaves coming north. It was built like a rock, but all from timber. The maze of rooms was so complex that I often thought it was the kind of house murders were committed in and never discovered. Portions of the structure had been built in the mid-1800s and were a proverbial tinderbox: wooden beams, lamb's-wool insulation, wallpaper everywhere, and carpet and furniture waiting to be consumed.

Dick's meager efforts to extinguish the fire with a garden hose were of no consequence, as the entire home would be at risk within minutes.

"Where the hell are the fire trucks?" Dick yelled, losing in his efforts to retard the flames.

"A few more minutes," Diane called back. "They couldn't find the address."

"Jesus. It's only one of the biggest houses in Massillon," Dick muttered in bewilderment.

Some relief came when the trucks finally pulled onto the property and up the hill to the house.

"Where's the hydrant?" they heard one of the men calling to the other.

"I don't know," came the sad reply.

And the fiasco continued with a desperate search, covering several acres immediately surrounding the house, for a hydrant. The fire had now jumped permanently from the pool house to the main living quarters. A call back to the station for tanker trucks took more minutes they didn't have. By then, the glow could be seen all over Massillon. When the tanker trucks arrived, the firefighters could only manage the flames from the outside. The house was history.

It was cold and damp as Diane ran in panic from the fire, one-quarter mile down the hill, falling many times, scraping her arms and legs on the debris from the trees. She did anything to escape the flames—and maybe she even ran harder to escape the emotional confinement of the relationship.

Patty stayed with her dad, standing and watching the drama of their house going up in flames, awed and speechless at the magnificence of the destruction. Nothing could be done as she clutched her father's waist in shock.

"Where's your wife?" a fireman asked Dick, interrupting their mesmerized trance.

"She was here, but now I don't know." His head turned in all directions as if he expected her to be within feet of him and Patty.

"Is she clear of the house?" the fireman asked with some alarm.

"Yes, I carried her out myself," Dick replied.

The fire was at a maintenance stage, freeing up several men to fan out in an attempt to locate Diane. It had been thirty minutes. They were concerned, as they knew that panic can cause erratic behavior—many times leading to broken bones or other bodily harm. The estate had over forty acres where Diane could be. They searched frantically for some time and found nothing.

Then they heard her, crying out for help in a diminished, childlike manner. She was lying in the swale alongside Valerie Lane in nothing more than her nightgown, some distance from the house, shivering and pathetic in her despair.

When the ambulance came, Dick tried to console her, but all she could say was, "This is all your fault! This is your family, and it's all your fault."

The words hung there as an indictment for all to hear, not specific in their meaning but heart wrenching in their incrimination.

Patty went to stay with her grandparents, and the only call Mike received at the academy was from Grandpa: "Mike, there's been a fire. The house is gone. Everyone's okay. Don't worry."

Economy of words can be a sharp knife cutting away at natural emotions wanting to be expressed. Neither of Mike's parents thought to call and help him process his concerns over what had happened.

Dick stayed away from the hospital for three days, with Diane suspecting Dick was with the other woman the entire time. In reality, Dick told me at a later time that he had lost total respect for Diane and considered her pitiful display during the fire to be completely unwarranted.

* * *

I was in Chicago that Monday after Thanksgiving. There was a big reorganization meeting for Xerox's Midwest Region offices. I was one of the district managers.

It was a "do not disturb" meeting, but a call came through for me. It was Carole.

"You've got to call Dick," she said with alarm.

"What's wrong?"

"They had a fire at their house—a bad fire."

"Whose house?" I asked. I wasn't sure if she was talking about my parents' home or my brother's home.

"Dick's house. Everything is gone!" She gave me a number for the motel where Dick could be reached. "He needs to talk with you."

I must have looked shocked. Tony, my boss, asked if I was all right.

"It's unbelievable," I said. "My brother's entire home is gone. Tony, this isn't just some tract home, but a twelve-thousand-square-foot turn-of-the-century mansion. I need to take a break and give him a call."

"Go," he said.

After I reached Dick and confirmed no one was hurt, he started to explain.

"It's all gone, burnt right to the ground. I've never seen anything like it—like a marshmallow in flames," he said. "As near as we can tell, the fire started in the pool house."

Later, it was determined that a malfunction in the new mechanical control system for the pool had caused a gas leak.

"We were lucky to get out," Dick said. "Patty is with Mom and Dad, and Mike left for the academy before the fire started. But Diane's in the hospital . . . they think it was a breakdown from her panic."

"What can we do? What do you need?" I said, not knowing where to begin.

"It's hard to explain, but we have nothing but the clothes we wore as we escaped the house."

This was big news in Massillon—a prominent family's disaster, a real-life Humpty-Dumpty metaphor complete with the elevation of their forty-acre estate being the highest in town. "The fire must have stood out like an orange ball in the night sky," Dick told me.

Yet simmering in the background was the growing reality that "all the king's horses and all the king's men" hadn't recognized that the impact of concussions from football could show up decades after the events. Those concussions had sparked a lifelong process of neuron degeneration—much more destructive than the house fire.

* * *

Two days before Christmas, with the family living in a rental home, Dick walked out.

"I can't do this anymore," he said to Mike.

Dick didn't come back until after New Year's Day. Mike had already returned to the academy, not seeing or talking with his dad before he left.

CHAPTER 10

The Dick we knew was gone . . .

In the spring of 1983, landscaping was the first order of business at our new home in Barrington, Illinois. It felt good to be back in the Midwest, closer to family. And regardless of the disruption with the fire and their marriage falling apart, Dick and Diane generously made the eight-hour drive from Canton in order to help out. Maybe they just needed a break.

Dick, Diane, and Patty arrived on Friday, towing a Bobcat with all the landscaping accessories on the trailer. Maybe it was our heritage of having a grandfather who was a florist or a father who couldn't say no to a project, but the do-it-yourself urge completely consumed Dick and me. Plans were made to plant over twenty trees with Dick's help that weekend. It was classic big-brother support as he jumped at the chance to pitch in. This was the Dick I always knew. The trees were already delivered, some of them large, and I was ready to go to work when they arrived that afternoon.

"Do you think the weather will hold out?" Dick immediately asked as he got out of the truck.

"Hi, Diane. Hi, Patty," I said, greeting them from their side of the truck and not wanting to get into business talk with Dick before acknowledging my favorite sister-in-law. "He seems eager to get started," I said after giving them both big hugs.

"You know Dick—always work," Diane responded cheerfully.

The beauty of Diane was that regardless of her frustration or disappointment, she always smiled. Or maybe it was the transcendent quality of her voice that made even the simplest disagreement sound like the second verse of a choir hymn.

"You're not going to hear me complain," I said. "Not many people have a brother with a Bobcat who will make the effort he has. Besides, Carole has plans to do some shopping that will keep you out of the way."

Finally, I turned back to Dick and responded to his original question. "No, I don't think the weather will hold out." I gestured toward the sky.

"We'd better get started, then. Show me what you've got planned," Dick said, taking charge.

We walked the one-acre, graded dirt terrain on the hilly property, identifying where each of the trees would go, all the while keeping our jackets zipped, as the damp air went right to the bone.

"Let's start while the dirt is dry. Some of these side-hill spots will get tricky when the rain turns everything to mud," Dick said from experience.

It didn't take Dick long to unload the trailer and the Bobcat. He fired it up and began distributing trees to their planting locations around the lot. And true to our forecast, it started to rain. At first it was light, but then it picked up. Dick was working the equipment like a madman, digging holes, positioning trees, and refilling the dirt as quickly as humanly possible. I was on the ground doing my best to ensure they were straight before getting backfilled.

Years later, Dick told me a story about his trip to South Korea while representing Daewoo, a competitor to Bobcat. This was after he lost his Bobcat dealership. Daewoo engineered good skid-steer equipment, but their representatives didn't know how to sell and demonstrate the product in the United States. They asked him to show them what the equipment could do on a large, steep pile of dirt their own engineers were afraid of scaling. After years of hands-on customer experiences with Bobcats, from mining to construction to farming, this was a piece of cake. Dick smiled as he told me how they were in awe of his handling of their equipment, well beyond the level of their own engineers.

Afterward, he played some baseball with their employee team, and to say the least, they were again impressed. "They thought I was a superstar," he told me.

Watching him maneuver the Bobcat that weekend in the rain—on the hilly, slick, muddy surfaces of the yard—I could see why the story made sense. He was a superstar when it came to operating the equipment under any conditions. He was efficient, fast, and all business.

By 11:00 that night, we finally took a break for dinner. We were exhausted and hungry, but with only 50 percent of the trees in. We showered, changed, and ate dinner at 11:30.

"You're going to be happy we got this much done when you see the mud tomorrow," he said while drinking a glass of milk.

I had been the cold, exhausted, grunt-labor guy on the ground the whole time, and now I was halfway through a six-pack to ease the muscle soreness setting in. "I gotta hand it to you," I said. "I was worried the project wouldn't get done with the rain forecast. You really know what you're doing."

"Most people only use my Bobcats for one type of job, so they don't get the experience I do. Every time I get in one, it's a new customer with a new project, so I've learned a lot. The equipment has become an extension of my body, like another set of arms and legs. At forty, I'm young for an operator, but I don't think anyone else would have accomplished what we did today."

The next day, it poured—pretty much a washout for doing work. We played board games in the morning, and the girls went shopping in the afternoon. Our hope for a break in the weather produced no results. We went to five o'clock Mass and then to dinner at Bacchus Nibbles, a favorite local place where we could sit next to the fireplace. We talked of family, Michigan State football, and, of course, the remainder of the project to be finished.

"It's hard to say how much we'll finish tomorrow . . . depends on the rain tonight," Dick said while actually sipping a glass of Chardonnay. This was a rare moment when Dick eased his temperate attitude toward alcohol. I took that as a good sign.

"I'm glad to see you're loosening up a bit, Dick," Carole said, acknowledging the Chardonnay. She offered a toast to how appreciative we were of their help, specifically Dick's contribution. It was genuine, and I believe Dick truly felt grateful.

When they left Sunday afternoon, I still had some Bobcat work to finish, but it was the easy stuff.

"Rent a unit for a half a day to get the work done," Dick said before leaving. "It will do you good to learn how the equipment works. It may even change your life as to how you approach projects like this."

Maybe, maybe not, I thought. *But one thing is for sure: this project would never have gotten finished without Dick's generous help.*

The next day, I went to the local trophy shop and had them customize a "Big Brother of the Year" award that was prominently displayed in Dick's office during our next visit to Canton. His acceptance of my praise was genuine and validating.

But the positive feelings from working together that weekend disappeared as Carole dropped a bomb soon after they left—Diane had confided in her that their marriage was not likely to survive. We were dumbfounded, but we admitted that seeing them once or twice a year was not enough to notice the problems. It was incredulous to me that Dick would accept being divorced, as this was completely off track from our Catholic upbringing and the brother I grew up with. *How could he change so much?* I thought.

Dick later told me the marriage probably never should have taken place at all—a rationale that allowed for an eventual annulment. He would rather dissolve the marriage's very existence than face the defeat of a divorce. Nothing made sense.

Diane spent New Year's with Carole and me in Barrington—alone.

* * *

Early in 1983, Dick was well into an extended rebuilding effort of their home with the insurance money. It was to be a seventeen-thousand-square-foot estate complete with tennis court, indoor pool, racquetball court, and a dedicated music room for the grand piano. It resembled an executive retreat center. The new house was positioned roughly on the same footprint as the old one—on the highest vantage point for miles in Massillon. From the front cobblestone deck, the magnificent view captured your attention, overlooking the estate, the valley, and the surrounding countryside.

Dick and Patty moved into the house in the spring of 1984. Their time together went fast with Patty's school and sports, Dick's focus on the business, and the vast array of projects connected with the new house.

With the annulment process well under way, Paula moved in the following year.

Dick met Paula during a skiing vacation in Vail. She had grown up in East Saint Louis, was married at sixteen, and was divorced shortly after. She got pregnant with Valerie; a son, Gary, soon followed. Grandma raised the kids while Paula worked. She married again, but the new husband supposedly forbade her to acknowledge her kids as her own at their country club. She divorced a second time.

Paula brought a certain way of life to the house—not all bad, as she was a creative homemaker and cook and tried to win Patty over. The positive chemistry between Dick and Paula was genuine at the beginning and good for Dick.

But then Paula's family migrated into the house. Valerie—pregnant with Bridget and unmarried—moved in, only to be followed by Gina, Paula's niece. Valerie went on to have another child, Derek, as well. According to Patty, the only good to come of the migration was Paula's mother, but she died one month after moving in. Dick had become completely surrounded by streetwise women who knew how to get what they wanted from a man. The new estate became more of a halfway house for Paula's family than a home.

It was an overwhelming time for Patty, yet in some ways, her experience growing up was easier than Mike's, not being the firstborn male. But she suffered through her high school years under the stress of a shattered Camelot marriage. Despite everything, she loved her dad. As Paula's family took over, though, Patty saw her dad lowering his standards. "Their background is not what I'm used to," she once said.

* * *

Carole and I came to visit Dick and meet Paula not long after she moved in.

"It'll never be the same," Dick said.

"What do you mean? It's phenomenal," Carole said, referring to the spectacular new house.

"That's not it. All the pictures and mementos are gone . . . lost in the fire. I didn't think I would miss them as much as I do."

"Why didn't you say so? We've got plenty of pictures you can have," Carole offered.

"That won't work anymore."

"Why not?"

"Paula's pretty protective of her turf, and I don't think pictures of my former life would go over well."

"Dick, that's ridiculous," Carole chimed in with attitude.

Paula did bring out a more positive, fun side of Dick

we hadn't seen in some time. But her lack of boundaries and our growing awareness of her materialism and skewed moral compass disgusted both of us.

"Neither she nor you can ignore your previous life," Carole said. "That won't be healthy for you, and for sure not Patty and Mike."

"It's the way it is," he responded.

Around that time, I started noticing a distant look in Dick's expression, a flat affect that was new, at least to me. I thought it was sadness.

"Plus," he said, "I don't know if I ever told you, but when the fire happened, nobody in this community ever volunteered to help us . . . Not one phone call . . . no one!"

"That can't be," we both said in unison.

"You've lived here all your life!" I added.

"Well, it can be. Not the church, not personal friends, or family friends . . . no one, despite the money and favors I've helped people with through the years. If it weren't for Mom and Dad still living here, it wouldn't feel like home at all."

"You sound angry. And personally, I don't blame you," I said.

"I am, and it's causing me to look at my life here differently."

"What do you mean?" Carole asked.

"I've spent too much time doing everything for the team—everyone else. Now I'm going to focus on me."

It was a disturbing comment. In the past, Dick's definition of *team* may have been an actual athletic team, the family team, or just the team of he and I doing things together. But more and more, I recognized a shift in his values, where the reference to *team* was really a need to be grounded in personal achievement. It was actually a cry for help. From that point forward, *team* became synonymous with *I*—a closed-loop, self-fulfilling ideology.

His world continued to shrink. This was new thinking, a different Dick from what I knew. He began calling himself Richard, as Paula had so cleverly crafted. He was 180 degrees from his roots. "Dick" was the brother I loved, but "Richard"—or "King Richard," as some referred to him—had evolved way out of proportion. The Dick we knew was gone. He had become a tool to be manipulated by others.

Was this a crossbreeding of Dick's self-focus, the pathology of CTE, and the influence of Paula's avarice? As far as we could see, he had zero ability to say no to the materialistic demands of Paula and her family.

CHAPTER 11

Dick's world was a treadmill of
defensive maneuvers as he tried
to outrun his bad decisions.

Dick's decision-making had taken a one-eighty. He had created a cycle of dependency: Dick's need to feel superior was fueled by people who needed him to meet all their wants. The King Richard ego spiraled out of control. In contrast, Dick saw only defiance in Patty's and Mike's growing independence, even though he had insisted so much upon it. In some ways, he may have felt rejected by them.

To Dick and Paula's credit, they did make a big effort in visiting Mike at the Naval Academy. Dick was very proud of Mike. He sang in one of the navy choral groups performing throughout the United States and did well in his studies as an engineering student. Yet when Mike came home for visits, the relationship returned to ground zero.

Mike never saw the new house as a home. Built to Dick's design, the outrageous display of over-the-top appointments raised red flags about Paula's obvious attraction to Dick's wealth. The kitchen looked like a department store with hundreds of floor decorations—families of porcelain ducks and chickens, a manger farm setting, and more. There were dozens of sixty-four-ounce drink cups filled with coins, baskets with thousands of tennis balls, closets jammed with clothes, too many fur coats, an office stacked with paper—excess and consumption. *Who needs this and why?* Mike thought. Not too many years later, Dick and Paula would also add twenty-six weeks of time-shares at five separate properties, multiple homes, four boats, and a garage full of stuff that was never used.

Mike graduated from the academy in 1986, the same year Patty graduated from Central Catholic. Patty left for Ohio University, where she majored in business and graduated four years later. The first week Patty returned home after graduating, Dick told her to move out. "Get a job," he said. Bridget, Paula's granddaughter, had already taken over Patty's bedroom. Patty moved to Hilltop Properties, an apartment complex Dick owned, and then left after finding a job three months later.

Patty bitterly remembers the hard line her dad took in insisting she make her own way. Though it did help her become independent, it felt like a double standard. With Paula's children and grandchildren, it was a constant trail of dependence and handouts, with Dick footing the bill all the way. Dick showed his love by giving things, and Patty showed her love by living up to his expectations of independence—a rock and a hard place.

For Mike, the big moment of separation came when he did not accept the offer to ultimately take over the business. Dick had the papers drawn up in advance, with no consultation or involvement from Mike.

"Dad, it's just not what I want to do with my life," Mike said after Dick presented the documents.

Dick just sat there, rejected, with a sad look on his face, as if he had failed. He had made independence a priority for Mike and Patty their whole lives. But now that they were independent, he had lost control. It was an eventual by-product of insisting on a focus emphasizing his own footsteps instead of their interests and their future.

* * *

Living in Chicago made it hard for Carole and me to stay on top of Dick's situation. We would see them once, rarely twice, a year. Most frequently, it was during our trips to Ohio over long Thanksgiving weekends. Seeing Dick in the same setting each year was like *Groundhog Day*. Being together only when repeating the same holiday rituals made it harder to see his changes.

But we did notice a lack of friendships on Dick's part. My high school friendships were intact, but Dick's friends were nonexistent, even though they and he lived in the community where we grew up. The odd way he clung to me and my high school friends indicated the lack of a developed social network of his own.

On a good note, Paula did add a social context to "Richard's" life. She claimed he truly was the love of her life, and at that time, I believed it. The fun, athletic, and extroverted side of her personality facilitated the development of a codependent social network outside his business setting. Regardless of our distrust of Paula's motives, she did seem good for him.

We were happy when we were invited along with Dick and Paula to a Lake Cable home of one of Paula's friends.

Two other couples joined us as well. The evening involved dinner and cocktails in their beautiful home, with the men retiring to the poolroom for some competition. It was a game I had developed some skill at—Dick and I were partners.

I think the host was more than a little frustrated by losing. So when Dick said, "How big is this table, anyway?" the host overreacted.

"What's the matter, Richard—isn't the table big enough for you?" The sarcasm and jealously was out of line.

I felt bad for Dick, as his intent certainly hadn't been to upstage our host. As a comment, it was innocent enough. I knew Dick was considering a table for their home. However, having completely monopolized the earlier conversation with details of over-the-top design features in his new home didn't help Dick's case. Dick still had a reputation for self-focused conversation.

The evening ended soon thereafter. In the car, Paula asked what happened. I explained, trying to cover for Dick, but it was Dick who said, "I don't intend to apologize for my success. If they can't handle my comments, that's their problem."

So it was with Dick. As his world shrunk, his insensitive persona—his need to focus only on himself and his need to be better, just as it was in high school—grew out of proportion. He lacked a filter for social context, ultimately offending people far more than he had in high school. And then his defensiveness backlashed, which caused him to carry a basically negative attitude toward their social network. He had become irritable, suspicious, and angry with almost everyone.

Returning home from the dinner party that night, I had my first realization of how this pattern was spiraling out

122

of control. *Why has it not corrected itself?* I thought. *Surely Dick is mature enough and confident with his achievements and success in business by now.*

I began to notice strange new behaviors when talking with Dick on the phone. All I had to do was say, "Hi, Dick," and he would be off—a nonstop, multilevel diatribe about anything and everything affecting him. He had become distrustful of the world around him. Dialogue digressed into monologue, with no pause or interplay in the discussion. I literally put the phone on the counter one evening, only to come back occasionally and say, "Is that right?" That went on for nearly a half hour. He finished, said, "Thanks for calling," and hung up.

"He's either hiding something or hiding from something," I told Carole afterward.

"Maybe both," she answered.

"Regardless, I don't think he knows what to do. It's as if he's losing control. Hell, I don't know what he needs. He doesn't seem able to listen."

* * *

Of greater concern was Dick's continuing dark side that seemed to completely defy his early adulthood value system. The orbitofrontal cortex (OFC) is one region of the brain damaged by a traumatic brain injury or concussion. Destruction of the OFC can create a pattern of disinhibited behavior—excessive swearing, hypersexuality, poor social interaction, out-of-control gambling, and poor empathizing ability. Unfortunately, we didn't understand this until years later. At that time, all we had were our reactions to Dick's outward behavior.

Dick's persona, public and private, had become his Achilles' heel. He required constant reinforcement. His growing insecurity was a target for anyone wanting an advantage over him. Decision-making lacked critical-thinking skills. Relationships became parasitic.

He developed an interest in Bobbie Jean—or BJ, for short. She was Paula's "wounded duck" friend, divorced by her husband three months after moving into the Massillon area. With Dick's poor decision-making and vulnerability to hardship-case women, it wasn't long before he had a key to BJ's apartment as she weaseled her way into his life and his wallet.

Business matters also degraded quickly for Dick, as extremely poor judgment became a regular occurrence. An attack-oriented coping mechanism didn't help. Some-where, Dick learned it was okay to make excuses, lie, or set others up, only to capitalize on their mistakes—all so he could avoid paying his obligations. "I'm not paying for that," he said over and over. Even Carole and I noticed this trait when he didn't pay our friends for a two-week rental of their lakeshore mobile home in Minnesota. It wasn't until I intervened that they got paid—six weeks later, with some excuse about forgetting.

With the source of the house fire determined to be a gas leak in the pool's control system, C. R. Kurtz, the electrical contractor responsible for the mechanical installation, was culpable. In the process of settling the lawsuit, Dick gained control of C. R. Kurtz and ran the owner off, destroying his future. (In conflicting rumors, some thought Cindy's cop-boyfriend may have actually started the fire, but there was no substantiating evidence.)

Mid-States became a house of cards in collapse. When Dick bought Mid-States, it had millions in the pension fund. But according to employees, he paid out only the minimum and removed the rest to "invest" in a fifty-eight-foot Catalina yacht moored at Hilton Head, South Carolina, where he and Paula had a time-share. The financial assistant at Mid-States brought nonbusiness purchases, such as the boat, to Tim Helline's attention, yet nothing was done. Employees threatened a class action but didn't follow through because they thought they'd lose their jobs. In the end, all residual monies were lost.

Employees allegedly believed the new Mid-States' computer system was intentionally sabotaged to destroy records that could incriminate Dick in claims of fraud and default by the IRS and Clark Equipment. Bobcat inventory was hidden from audits using false paperwork and Uniform Commercial Code documentation. This allowed the equipment in question to be used under the 0 percent flooring agreement to generate rental income at Timken, while financed at First National. Nine months of free money was created, and all IRS obligations avoided.

Dick had been responsible for the design and installation of such computer systems while at IBM. And was it a coincidence that the paper backup files were destroyed in the house fire? In time, Kathy, who handled the computer system, was replaced by Paula. Around the same time, security deposits from the Hilltop apartment complex, owned by Dick and managed by Paula, were rumored to have disappeared. Dick occasionally discussed all these issues with me under the incredulous assumption that he was being screwed.

Dick's world was a treadmill of defensive maneuvers

as he tried to outrun his bad decisions. And it seemed that everyone close to Dick was taking advantage of his situation. As he scrambled to keep the ship afloat, the rats were fleeing with carpetbags full of everything they could carry. At that time, his net worth was over $12 million. Over the next twenty years, it dwindled to nothing.

* * *

I was surprised to learn of Dick's tarnished reputation when I was in Canton on a consulting project, doing a needs-assessment at a leading public accounting firm. While interviewing each of the partners, I was ultimately confronted with the comment, "We need to know if you run your business like your brother runs his." I was shocked by the implication, and the partner offered only a vague reference to "ethics" as an explanation.

I knew Dick was aggressive in his business, but that was all I could confirm. It was the first time I became concerned about the impact on our family name—a reputation my parents earned through years of hard work, community support, and fair treatment.

I confronted Dick. "What's this about?"

"They're just upset because I moved my financial-support needs to a larger Cleveland accounting firm," he replied, dismissing it.

I wanted to defend Dick but also protect the Proebstle reputation. I was very concerned but felt confused and trapped in my inability to intervene.

CHAPTER 12

"There's something wrong with Dick,"
my dad told Carole on his deathbed.
"Mom and I are worried."

Family drama escalated the summer of 1988 with the shocking announcement that Dad had pancreatic cancer. Mom had already been relegated to in-home bed care due to her Alzheimer's and Parkinson's diagnosis. Dad had been her sole caretaker for two years. The stress on him was 24-7. We moved Mom to a nursing facility for Alzheimer's and Parkinson's only after Dad's illness reduced his capacity to care for her. He would have it no other way.

Paula displayed a rare and remarkable willingness to intervene with both parents' many daily needs. On our various trips throughout the summer, we saw evidence of the ravaging effects on Dad's body, and we knew he wouldn't last long.

"There's something wrong with Dick," my dad told Carole on his deathbed in August. "Mom and I are worried."

Dad's unconditional love for Carole was obvious. He had thrived on the banter of Carole's differing points of view. Dad loved an argument, and he loved and trusted

Carole for her independent thinking. This comment was Dad's last attempt at course correction for a son. Nothing really came of the discussion, however. It was painful for him to talk, and Carole didn't have the framework to ask the right questions.

As I discussed this scene with Carole years later, I don't think Dad made that comment just because of Dick's personality. After all, they lived close to Dick and saw everything firsthand. I believe that Dad, without having a name for it, was speaking to the destructive forces at work with Dick's behavior—the ongoing progression of CTE.

It was as if Dick no longer controlled his own decisions. Consumed by the need for profits at Mid-States and controlled by Paula's influence, Dick was a different person. His own children were now virtually excommunicated from his life, much as the annulment had done with Diane. Carole and I pulled away as well. He had become something of an idiot savant, with no friends and an obsession for money. There's nothing wrong with being financially successful, but this simply wasn't the person I knew, loved, and grew up with.

* * *

Mom died on October 9, 1990, and the turnout of friends and family for the funeral was a tribute to her wonderful and unselfish nature in dealing with people. Her sister Irene had died earlier in the week, making it difficult for everyone in the extended family.

For Dick, it was time to reflect. The tremors in his writing hand, the memory losses, and the noticeable inconsistencies in his behavior created the concern that he was possibly being affected by Alzheimer's and/or Parkinson's. We were told it wasn't a hereditary condition, but even our grandmother died from Parkinson's. That Dick had an early onset condition made sense, but he was reluctant to discuss it. To my knowledge, Paula never pressed the issue for Dick to seek medical advice at this stage.

"Who are these great-grandchildren in the obituary?" Uncle Bill, Mom's brother, asked me the day before Mom's funeral, apparently at the behest of the other brothers and sisters. They were generous and forgiving people, but not stupid, and they were extremely protective of their sister, who had suffered the effects of Alzheimer's and Parkinson's for four years.

"Who do you mean?" I asked. Details had never been a strength of mine. With Dad now gone for over two years and the emotion of preparing Mom's eulogy, this inclusion about great-grandchildren in the obituary had been missed.

"Well, it says in the obituary that there are two great-grandchildren. Who are they?" Uncle Bill asked again.

Bill was very bright, with dark hair and blue eyes, and was the second youngest of the McDermott clan. There were three sisters and three brothers—a remarkably interesting, successful, and loyal group all raised through the late '30s and '40s by our grandmother, Julia. She was a single mother due to a rail-yard accident that killed our grandfather. The family went into survival mode, living in Grand Forks, North Dakota—which I'm sure accounted for an attention to detail when family tree connections were being made.

"They have to be Paula's grandchildren," Aunt Margaret said.

"You mean Bridget and Derek?" Carole said.

"If that's their names. But she and Dick aren't married, are they? And besides, they would be step-grandchildren."

This created a burr under everyone's saddle, as the family knew Paula had been using the Proebstle name as her own for some time, despite the fact that she and Dick weren't married. For a while, she even tried to pass off her grandkids as her own children so as not to appear older. Carole and I had been aware of various deceptions for a while.

"You're not going to believe this," Carole said that night while getting ready for bed. "Paula was born in 1937! She's five years older than Dick!"

"How did you find that out?" I said, though not doubting the information. We knew she had been falsely passing herself off as being near Dick's age or even younger.

"I looked in her purse."

Carole, always motivated by truth, was embarrassed. But the temptation to look at Paula's driver's license while her purse was left unattended in the kitchen had been beyond her ability to resist, considering Paula's track record for falsehoods.

"You *what*?"

"It was just lying there, and I couldn't stop myself," she said with the gleeful grin of a ten-year-old telling on a sibling. "You know how I have to have the truth."

"It would have been very embarrassing, had you been caught."

"I had to know. And I'll bet there are a lot more lies to that woman."

Our dislike for Paula escalated. Dick's diminished thinking capacity, dependency, and need for attention and praise came with a healthy price tag. His inability to see her manipulation was completely naïve and not like Dick. He had become unable to protect himself. In truth, it appeared he had begun a pattern of robbing Peter to pay Paul in the business in order to maintain Paula's need for appearances.

She had milked Dick for over twenty fur coats—"gifts," she called them. There wasn't a fur-bearing animal on the planet that hadn't been sacrificed for her wardrobe. The jewelry she coaxed out of Dick was stunning but way beyond acceptable—completely out of place for the Canton-Massillon community. On sunny days, she drove around town in a pearl-white Stutz Bearcat convertible Dick had also "given" her. Needless to say, it got attention and created gossip—as if there were a need to create more talk.

When Dick told me he was marrying her, I said, "I think I have the right to say something. I know you're not looking for my permission to marry Paula, so I'll just say what I have to say, particularly seeing as you asked for my written input to your annulment with Diane."

Dick knew what was coming.

"Marrying Paula will be a mistake, Dick, and she'll take you for everything you're worth."

They married anyway. As you might guess, our face time with them declined dramatically going forward.

* * *

Dick and I still communicated by phone, especially regarding the distribution of our parents' estate. Dick had been appointed as executor, which seemed bizarre, but it was a long-standing decision my parents had made when his business skills were more intact.

The estate was modest, and his approach as executor was not forthcoming. Questions arose, particularly when we started to discuss the property on Leech Lake in Minnesota.

Dad and Mom had developed the virgin land and built the original cabin as a summer place for their retirement. As I write this very chapter, I am sitting in the rebuilt version of that cabin, which serves as a North Star to our family tradition. It's a beautiful virgin forest and lakeside home now positioned on seventeen acres—sand shoreline and perfectly located to enjoy all of Leech Lake. My own grandchildren tell me I would face certain expulsion from the family if we ever sold the place.

"Dick, what happened to our idea of building something together?" I said on the phone.

He and I had always felt that a combined approach, involving both our families, would make good use of the original twenty-seven-acre lakeshore property and encourage the tradition in Minnesota to go forward in the next generation.

John was very clear that he had no interest in the Minnesota property, partly because of his independence and partly because of Minnesota's distance from their home in Warren, Pennsylvania. I tried to keep all three of us brothers involved with a letter to John, but to no avail.

As it turned out, Dick had other plans up his sleeve as well.

"I decided I just want the narrow pie-piece shape on the north end. I'm not convinced I'll use it as much as I thought."

This sounded like Paula talking, as she struggled with

the up-north wilderness setting—not enough glitz.

"So what are you going to do?"

"I was able to buy a few acres next to the property, which makes the pie piece more usable."

"What do you mean?" I asked, now getting a little suspicious. There had been other irregularities in his handling of the estate, making it necessary for me to keep a close eye on his progress. I started to pace more than normal in my office as we talked.

"Much of the shoreline on the pie piece isn't usable, as it doesn't have enough depth. So I negotiated a purchase of the twelve acres behind it to provide for enough property to develop."

I couldn't believe his deceitfulness. "Dick, you did all of this while you were executor."

"So?" he replied with condescending disdain.

"That's a complete conflict of interest! Plus, you and I were talking about trying to keep the property together for family purposes. You've been lying to everyone. Did you talk with John about what you were doing?"

"John and I don't talk much."

"That's your job, Dick—to keep people informed. But you used your private knowledge as executor to make a decision that completely favored you, regardless of the impact on the rest of the family. That's not right."

"It's done now," he said as if to cut off the conversation.

"You may have purchased the other property, but the settlement of the estate isn't done." My voice escalated as I dug in. "What's the name and telephone number of the estate attorney you're using in Cleveland?"

"I don't see how that's any of your business."

"I'm making it my business as one of the heirs." The

conversation was on a collision course. "We're either going to reapportion the value of the Leech Lake land, or I'm going to call the attorney and file a complaint about your mishandling of the assets."

"You can't do that."

"Watch me!"

The silence on both ends was deafening. I knew Dick had apportioned the property based on the low value of the pie-piece shape, but the added land had changed the piece's value dramatically.

"What we're going to do is value your pie piece at the same value as the remainder of the property. If you don't like it, give me the phone number to call."

"That's not fair," Dick said.

"No, Dick, the way you've treated your brothers isn't fair."

Once the estate was ultimately rebalanced, the liquid asset payout shifted more favorably to John as well. Years later, Dick would complete the sale of his Leech Lake land at about twenty times the reapportioned inheritance value.

SECTION III

CTE OUTCOME—YOUR
BRAIN LOSES CONTROL

CHAPTER 13

Odd, "one-off" events also started
happening with greater regularity.

It was July 1997, and the "Cousin-Fest II" reunion at Leech Lake was wrapping up. The Proebstle cousins from John's, Dick's, and my family had traveled great distances to participate in this second-annual ritual that defined everything Proebstle: the love of competition. John and Peg were unable to make it, yet Paula was there. It would be her last.

For the three-day tournament, I—more formally referred to as "the Committee"—designed several events that would frustrate and challenge players—physically, emotionally, and intellectually. It was a fun way to reacquaint the cousins, and the name of the winning cousin would be forever revered on a gold chip on the official Cousin-Fest Trophy sitting on the cabin's fireplace mantel.

Jeff had won Cousin-Fest I but was dethroned by Jennifer, his sister, this week at Cousin-Fest II. Her win came under protest, as Jennifer had hired a professional fishing guide to help her catch the fifteen-pound northern pike that locked her victory in the all-important fishing segment. "Unfair," everyone claimed. The Committee ruled otherwise, as there was no penalty for creativity and initiative.

Dick and Paula left for Canton early on Sunday morning, the day after the games were over. Later that morning, just after they left, we were rudely interrupted by a knock.

"I want to talk with Dick Proebstle," said a local road contractor as he stood right outside our cabin door.

I hadn't seen this man in years. Someone, I presumed his brother, hovered off to the side in our backyard, about ten feet to my left in my periphery.

In a remote setting like this, it was unusual for someone to approach a home so directly without first alerting the occupants, typically with a small beep of the horn or by calling out. With the rural, private nature of most properties, it's generally considered polite behavior to give a wide berth. People spook easily, and they all have guns.

I stepped outside to talk.

"Do you know who I am?" the contractor demanded. His short, stocky frame looked a lot like one of the bulldozers he owned. His brutish reputation was well deserved.

"No, I don't." This guy was a bully. I wasn't about to acknowledge his existence by indicating I knew who he was. He didn't exist in my book.

After introducing himself, he said, "I'm the guy your fuckin' brother stole money from when I did his road."

"Don't know anything about it."

With a sneer, he explained something about how he had cleared out the new entrance Dick built for his property. But the road had crossed into someone else's property. Dick got sued for taking down trees on the other person's land, so he didn't pay this guy for his services. But the contractor argued differently, claiming Dick told him to clear the land

and therefore still owed him about $900.

"I came to collect," he said, "and I don't care if it's from you or him."

"Well, Dick already left, and I don't know what you're talking about, so you're sure not getting the money from me."

"Tell you what, Mr. Big Shot," he challenged. "I'll fight you for the money right here and now. You can even have the first punch, right here," he said, sticking his chin out while displaying a nasty expression.

"You're outta line," I replied. Squaring my shoulders, I started to walk him and his brother toward their truck.

"We got ways with people like you," the brother said, speaking for the first time. "That nice cabin of yours may just catch fire when you're not here. Now you better pay my brother what he's due."

My blood started to boil, but I didn't feel that a fight at my age was a good idea. I did truly wish this discussion had taken place twenty years earlier, however.

The brother started to circle me as we talked, positioning himself for a flank attack.

"Watch yourself," I said, holding his eye contact hard. He backed off.

"Don't look at him, look at me," the contractor said.

My heart pulsed.

As she listened and watched from inside the cabin, Carole realized I was about to lose it. She told Jeff, "Go out there and back your dad up."

Things cooled off immediately when Jeff walked outside and circled the brother. Jeff is six-four, 240, and his presence seemed to take the vinegar out of these brothers. Like all bullies, their steam fizzles when the sides even up. They retreated to their truck.

Once they were inside with the doors closed, I leaned on the open driver's window and said, "You may have issues with my brother keeping his word, but you won't with me. What I'm going to do right now is call the police and file a report. If I ever see you on my property again, it won't end so pleasantly."

They drove off without another word.

"Thanks, Jeff. Your timing was perfect."

"Does this happen often up here?"

"Never. Sometimes people are a little primitive as to how they handle things, but I've never had this happen."

"What was it about?"

"They claim they did work for Dick and never got paid. What pisses me off is that Dick and I had a conversation about this just a few weeks ago. I had heard rumors about bad blood between Dick and this man. I just didn't know the reason. I told him that if this was going to cause an issue during the reunion, he needed to fix it before things got out of hand. He obviously didn't. Damn poor judgment, I'd say."

This wasn't the first and wouldn't be the last dissatisfied businessperson looking to get even with Dick. But it was my first actual encounter in what Mike described as a developing pattern. I expressed my dissatisfaction about the situation in a letter to Dick and then a follow-up phone call.

On the phone, his only reaction was, "It's none of your business." His world continued to close in rapidly as defensive behavior and aggressiveness masked an inability to think through issues clearly. From Dick's perspective, others were out to get him.

Years later in 2004, Dick finally answered the letter. Dick used the word *I* thirty-six times on the first page alone.

It was an unmistakable cry for help. I wish I had recognized it. Instead, it just made me angrier.

* * *

Odd, "one-off" events started happening with greater regularity during this millennial period. On a 2001 trip to Minnesota, Dick's truck broke down near Midway Airport— not a good part of Chicago. It was a snapped engine belt.

Mike was to meet Dick at the lake, but he got the call to come early from Indiana to help. It was about 2:00 a.m. when Mike arrived and found Dick asleep in his truck at the side of the road. Somehow Dick had hitchhiked to an AutoZone earlier that evening to purchase a new belt. Then he had hunkered down, waiting for Mike to help install it. They slept in the van together and completed the job the next morning.

Once back on the Eisenhower Expressway, Dick side-swiped a car. As the patrolman wrote out the citation, Dick just stood there with that now-too-familiar blank look on his face.

After spending his week's vacation in Minnesota with his dad, Mike returned home. Dick spent several additional months—alone—developing his land on the Ottertail Peninsula. He had always talked about building a cabin for himself but never did. Consequently, he chose to live out of the back of his truck in a secretive fashion.

The more Dick worked on the land, the more fundamental he became. His hygiene, grooming, language skills, and social conduct plummeted. His basic instincts changed from those of an educated, successful businessman to those of a backwoods loner, revealing an animallike quality to his day-to-day existence. We all thought he had plenty of money at that time, so the primitive conditions to which he subjected himself appeared very strange.

When Dick did interact with someone, it was all about the progress he was making on the property. Otherwise, his behavior became more "in the shadows," so to speak, staying on the fringe of involvement and lacking the enthusiasm he had as a young man. It seemed as if his motives were largely fueled by a need for privacy and a fear that others were out to get him.

Throughout this period, Dick started having frequent panic attacks in addition to migraines. Anxiety is now recognized as one of twenty-six post-concussion symptoms. Most times, he thought he was having a heart attack and would admit himself to a hospital without telling the family.

Once when he was in Colorado after Mike and his wife, Melissa, had separated, Mike took Dick to a hospital during an attack, only to find out the attacks had been going on for years. Dick told Mike about going to the "happy place"—the hospital—to "calm my mind down." As near as we could tell, the hospital seemed to provide a safe harbor for Dick. It was clear the attacks were happening with more regularity. And later, in almost every phone conversation, Dick told Mike he felt tired and run-down all the time. But without any clear diagnosis for their father, Mike and Patty were in the dark.

It's easy to see, in retrospect, how Dick's undiagnosed dementia initiated a behavior pattern of confusion. His paranoia had become real, considering the business challenges, the lack of trust in his wife, and the many personal financial issues. In his thinking, he was alone in his battle.

CHAPTER 14

The truck contained a bed covered with dust—
much like a horse stall.
He had been calling it home.

It was late spring 2005—and colder than normal, even for Minnesota. Dick had just arrived on the peninsula to work on his land. There was no question that his box truck had become his permanent Minnesota residence. His marriage with Paula was, to say the least, strained with rumors of both having extramarital activities, financial squandering, and general disregard for family encounters. She was busy with her like-minded friends at the Hilton Head time-share. It was Paula's favorite of the twenty-six they owned.

Dick had an electric space heater for the truck. But for some unknown reason, rather than hooking it to his gas generator, he decided to pull into a neighbor's driveway and connect the heater directly to the electrical box on their cabin. Maybe he was just trying to avoid the constant noise of the running generator, but it was poor judgment. All hell broke loose when the owner, a retired cop from Des Moines, showed up unexpectedly to find Dick tapped into their utilities without permission.

When Carole and I arrived a few weeks later, fully intent on preparing for Cousin-Fest III, several neighbors confronted us with their indignation and proclamations about Dick's audacity. People piled on the "Who does he think he is?" bandwagon. It was a natural reaction. And there was no defending his growing list of odd behaviors and actions.

Mike arrived later in July for Cousin-Fest III, combining it with a week's worth of work with his dad. Unfortunately, working with his dad at the lake didn't create the special memory he had hoped for, as it was nothing but physical labor on Mike's part with Dick in the Bobcat. It was as if Mike were a lineman and his dad were the quarterback calling plays. And there were other, bigger problems as well.

As Mike related, "We were going to use the Bobcat to punch through the ice ridge on the shoreline to create an access easement for one of the lots. But when I looked at the survey to verify the correct location for the breech, I discovered that Dad had misread the survey map and was about to place the access in the wrong location."

During that same week, Dick had constantly reviewed every survey line location—to "show" Mike where everything was. But in fact, he had really been looking to Mike for validation. As they walked survey lines together, they frequently found where Dick had had staked out the property incorrectly.

Maybe Dad was at the source of the contractor fiasco a few years back after all, Mike thought.

*　*　*

"Dad, I need to talk with you. I think we have a problem," Jeff said quietly and out of Patty's and Mike's hearing range.

Cousin-Fest III was in full swing. This was the first family get-together since Cousin-Fest II in 1997. Competition between the Proebstle cousins and grandkids was not for bleacher bums. I smiled, suspicious of Jeff's motives. He was desperate to reclaim his glory, but under the new team format, Mike and his son, Andrew, were leading.

"You're not going to convince me to change the rules just because Mike and Andrew are kicking butt," I said.

I had to be tough, as the Proebstle mind-set was to stay in the game at all costs. If I gave in to Jeff—my own son, no less—my life as the favorite uncle would be history, and I would be summarily disbarred from ever being the Committee again. The Committee answers to no one and has power equivalent to that of the pope for those three days, a position rarely achieved in any other endeavor in life.

"No, I'm serious," he said without the normal twinkle of deception in his eye.

My smile fell. "Talk to me," I said.

"It's Uncle Dick. The scoring is getting pretty messed up."

"What do you mean?"

Dick's mobility, with a new hip, was minimal, so I had given him the job of scoring the annual quiz chronicling our family's involvement on the Ottertail Peninsula for three generations. My goal was to keep the family's history alive, and the quiz was a fun way to do that.

"None of the scores make sense." Jeff handed me his answer sheet, clearly showing that Dick had marked some right answers wrong and some wrong answers right.

"He's just messing with you," I said.

"I don't think so."

Jeff walked me over to where we could see Dick sitting at the scoring table—a card table set up in the shade of an ash tree by the lake. Dick had never been particularly organized, but the random scatter of the various answer sheets did catch my attention. Worse yet, he looked lost and confused as worried desperation accentuated his expression.

It hit me in the gut. I'd seen a similar facial affect on Mom's face when we first noticed her dementia issue. Carole and I had been playing bridge with Dad and Mom, and we noticed she couldn't count her cards any longer—a skill in which she had been notoriously talented.

We approached him. "Hey, Dick," I said lightheartedly. "We're having claims of favoritism in the scoring. I think what we need to do is to double-score everyone's answer sheets to make sure we check for ties. If it's okay with you, I'll get Carole to help with the job."

"Okay," he responded. Relief filled his face. "There are a few answer sheets where the handwriting is hard to make out, and I might have messed up."

"No sweat. Just finish up the ones you have left, then Carole will go through them and catch any differences."

Dick went back to finish scoring as I sought out Carole inside. I motioned to Jeff to tag along. Obviously, something was wrong, and Carole was best suited to check it out.

"Tell Mom what we saw with Dick."

As Jeff recounted our experience, Carole nodded with understanding. "How did he respond when you told him I would help?"

"Almost relieved."

"It's probably the stress of being around a lot of people," Carole continued. Until Mike arrived, it had only been Dick and his dog, Cinder, living in the back of his truck. And now the whole family was here.

Later in the afternoon, when the games were done for the day and there was a minute to breathe, I asked Carole what she discovered when she had sat down with Dick and the quizzes.

"Not much more than what you already observed," she said. "The mistakes were there, for sure, but he seemed completely unaware. It may have been a brief panic attack or nervousness, which he's had in the past. But once I sat down, he became chatty. One thing's for certain: all of his past isolation is not good for him. Maybe he felt left out? On the other hand, it's possible the mistakes could have come from distractions. Regardless, it does seem that a change has occurred . . . a level of simplicity in his behavior that wasn't there before."

"He's only sixty-three. Mom's Parkinson's and Alzheimer's diagnosis didn't come until . . . let me think for a minute . . ."

I racked my brain. When you have dementia in your family, you start to second-guess yourself when an answer doesn't come immediately. It's like performance anxiety, and then you think, *Is it happening to me too?*

"It was 1984 when we first noticed it. That would have made her seventy-three," I finished, slightly reassured with my successful math recall.

"Could be an early onset for Dick," Carole said.

"Maybe, but something's not right."

I went to visit with Dick out in our new screened-in porch after dinner, but he was already falling asleep in the recliner.

"You okay?" I asked gently to rouse him from his nap.

"This has really been a good day. Thanks for putting everything together."

"Glad it worked out. Are you going to have some of that ice cream and pie before we kick the board game activities into gear?"

"A bowl of ice cream . . . yes. But then I'm off to bed. Cinder needs to be fed, and I'm bushed."

He ate the ice cream, singularly focused on the task, without interaction or disruption. It reminded me, again, of our mom and the attention she gave her food when in the nursing home.

We walked back to his truck together, just about a hundred yards along the sandy shoreline of the bay, but it took at least ten minutes. The sun was setting with its brilliant orange against the blue of the lake and the green of the forest on the opposite shore.

As Dick walked, I noticed a shuffling that was more pronounced. I realized that most of my recent interactions with Dick had been not up close. He had been sitting in his Bobcat "calling plays." I hadn't seen him walk much—not at the end of the day, anyway.

More so, there was a tiredness in his expression. And maybe I was just seeing things clearly for the first time, but the three-day-old beard was totally unlike Dick.

What's happening? I thought.

"You're moving slow, big brother," I said. "Do you feel all right?"

"Too much time in the Bobcat . . . Legs don't seem to work as well."

"Maybe some walking each day would help . . . Don't you think?"

"Maybe, but I just don't have the time anymore."

I could hear Cinder, chained to his running stake, barking well in advance of us nearing the truck. *That dog would drive me nuts,* I thought. But Dick seemed really connected to the dog, regardless of its aggressive, antisocial behavior.

When Dick opened the door to the truck bed, I was appalled. It contained a bed and a small chest of drawers, both covered with dust—much like a horse stall. He and Cinder had been calling it home.

"This place is a pit," I said, probably with too much judgment in my tone.

"No one asked you. It works for Cinder and me."

"What I meant was, wouldn't you like it better if you stayed with us?"

"It's easier this way. No one to answer to." His look was firm, not inviting any further comment. "I need to feed Cinder and get some rest. It was a good day."

Then, with a small tear in his eye, he said, "Mom and Dad would be proud of what you've done with the old cabin."

I initially thought it was regret that I saw in his eyes. But afterward, I realized it was an expression of helplessness for not being able to follow through with his own plans to build. Regardless of what I saw, it was heartbreaking to see his dream evaporate.

CHAPTER 15

"I think a pathological change
has taken place . . .
it's much deeper,
as if his wiring is all messed up."

On the way home to Canton from Leech Lake in 2005, Dick stopped in the Twin Cities for a surprise visit with his old law school friend Terry Glarner and his wife, Val.

Terry had always noticed a drive to succeed in Dick that was greater than most of their friends'. "Happiness is from the inside out," Terry would tell Dick. He was concerned that Dick seemed to think more and more that happiness was from the outside in, with a focus on material achievement. Regardless, there was no doubt that the unsuccessful law school experience had left a hole in Dick's self-esteem that had never been filled.

Dick showed up unannounced at Terry and Val's home, with his yellow truck and Cinder, who wouldn't stop barking.

"Don't let him in the house," Val said emphatically before Terry answered the door. Val was battling cancer. She had little patience or energy for Dick's high-maintenance need for attention and the conversation imbalance—90 percent about Dick and 10 percent tacked on at the end for them.

"Dick, what a shocker," Terry said after answering the door.

Dick might as well as had come straight from the backwoods. He hadn't showered or shaved in some time, and his clothes smelled badly from body odor.

"I thought you'd like the surprise. I'm on my way to Ohio."

"This is a real treat," Terry said. "I'm afraid our best option for lunch is at one of the local restaurants, though. You remember that Val has cancer, don't you? Well, it continues to take her down, and today's a bad day. Is that okay?"

Terry's respect for "who Dick had been" never faltered, so he covered his tracks to make Dick feel welcome without inviting him inside. Terry was happy that at least Paula was not with him, as both he and Val detested the woman. "No comparison to Diane . . . a real step down," they said.

At the restaurant, Terry found a booth where they could talk away from people. But Terry found Dick hard to understand.

"It seems like you're slurring your words a lot," he said with concern. "Have you had a stroke?"

"It's those damn concussions," Dick replied. "I've never been able to shake 'em."

It was remarkable that forty-plus years after the football events, he continued to self-diagnose the concussions as the source of his migraines. Diane had held the same conclusions about the impact of his concussions since early in their marriage. And yet, this conclusion never penetrated any professional's logic during Dick's many medical evaluations.

Dick continued talking nonstop about his deals, his apartments, his IRS troubles with delinquent back taxes, and his failure at Mid-States. *He almost takes pride in being on the wrong side of everything*, Terry thought.

"Are you going to be all right, Dick? I mean, this stuff is serious. Maybe you should consider getting some help."

Terry had seen the early effects of Dick's concussions back in law school, and he was concerned about the life-long impact. He didn't know how to approach these obvious issues. As an attorney, he knew Dick was vulnerable. He shook his head about how Dick was approaching every-thing. *A complete lack of judgment*, he thought, *over pretty serious problems*.

Later, Terry told Val, "I think a pathological change has taken place in Dick. It's way beyond the competitive Dick we used to know. It's much deeper . . . as if his wiring is all messed up."

* * *

After Dick got home, Tim Helline called to share some good news—and maybe to also bury the hatchet, as his parting with Dick at Mid-State had not been on the best of terms.

When Dick chose to take on the Daewoo skid-steer line—despite having a noncompete agreement with Melroe, the corporate entity for Bobcat—it was the beginning of the end for Mid-States. Dick lost the dealership in 2000. Tim's relationship with Melroe remained solid as he filled a neces-sary role in unraveling the customer issues and corporate challenges Dick had created. Tim continued under a new distributorship arrangement in Canton.

On the phone with Dick, Tim announced he had been enshrined as the sixth person in the Bobcat Hall of Fame. He was justifiably proud and wanted to thank Dick for everything he had taught him about the business in the early days.

Dick's only reply was, "That should be me. I earned that trophy!"

"No 'congratulations,' 'glad I could help,' or whatever," Tim said to me later.

In the end, Tim still claimed to be a fan of Dick's, but the business chaos and Dick's medical decline prohibited any reconciliation between them. Nor did Tim ever receive acknowledgment from the one person who mattered most to him.

* * *

With Terry and Tim, Dick was likely expressing the pathological form of Timothy Leary's competitive-narcissistic personality disorder, which includes a blind selfishness, a frantic effort to impress, and a boastfulness and exhibitionism that becomes flagrant and irrational. In addition, Dick's CTE dementia, with its lack of effective filtering, likely facilitated this competitive-narcissistic condition.

In retrospect, had the NFL not buried Bennet Omalu's case study in the November 2006 issue of *Neurosurgery* for three years, concussion research could have had a much more effective jump start. Much of the study focused on Mike Webster, "Iron Mike" of the Pittsburgh Steelers, the foundation case proving CTE dementia was related to concussions. It wasn't until 2010 that a "Must Read for NFL Players" poster was posted in every NFL locker room, stating:

> *Traumatic brain injury may lead to problems with memory and communication, personality changes, as well as depression and the early onset of dementia. Concussions and conditions resulting from repeated brain injury can change your life and your family's life forever.*

CHAPTER 16

Every piece of property was in foreclosure,
under eviction notice, and with
federal and/or state tax liens filed.

It was early spring 2007, and it had been some time since Dick and I had talked. It was difficult to have meaningful dialogue over the phone. I just couldn't wrap my brain around what was really happening to him, and we were drifting further apart. Trying to put myself in Dick's shoes wasn't easy—like trying to assemble a thousand-piece jigsaw puzzle with lots of blue sky.

The phone rang. "Uncle Jim?" It was Mike. "Patty and I need to talk to you about Dad. Things are getting strange."

"What do you mean, strange?" I said.

"Let's get Patty on another phone, as well."

Mike and Patty were making a team effort to help their dad, as neither was quite sure what to do on their own. They were in Canton that weekend to help Dick with a garage sale at his home on Lawndale Road. Dick and Paula had purchased the home a few years back, after Dick lost the dealership and could no longer financially maintain the big house. Mike and Patty had spent the weekend helping Dick clean out the garage and sell some of the things no longer needed—old Bobcat equipment, furniture from the big house, artwork, and so on.

"It's hard to make sense of the pigsty Dad's living in," Patty said. "It's almost impossible to walk through the house, with all the papers and unopened mail stacked randomly on card tables, countertops, end tables—everywhere. All the stuff from the big house has been jammed into this house with no thought. Nothing's been thrown away in a long time. It's so bad that it's impossible to clean . . . I wouldn't know where to begin."

"And it's no better in the garage out back," Mike chimed in. "It's stuffed with crap that's been in storage since Grandma and Grandpa died. Everything is full of mildew . . . just junk."

"Where's Paula?" I asked.

"In Hilton Head, where else?" Patty replied with that tone implying Paula's general lack of concern over anything that didn't directly affect her. "Dad's here by himself. We've sold a few of the things, but we're still not sure what to do next."

"Put your Dad on," I said.

In a few minutes, Dick was on the phone, full of braggadocio about selling things at their garage sale for "close to twelve thousand dollars." Many of his sentences weren't complete—just fragments of thought.

"When does Paula get back?" I asked.

"I think on Sunday."

Since it *was* Sunday, his reply wasn't very convincing.

Mike needed to get back to work in Warsaw, and Patty's flight for Pennsylvania was leaving that afternoon, so I cut the call short. "I'll call you back tomorrow after

Paula's home. You kids need to get going. We can talk more at that time."

When Mike and Patty came back on the line, I asked, "Do you guys think your dad will be okay on his own until tomorrow, if need be?"

"I think so," Patty said. "I can make him some food before I leave. Mike can feed Cinder. It looks like he sleeps on his La-Z-Boy in front of the TV, so there's not much else to do."

"Do the best you can. I'll pay a visit early tomorrow afternoon."

"Should we leave a note for Paula that you're coming?"

"No. No notes, no phone messages. Neither Dick nor Paula need to know I'm coming." My instincts told me a surprise visit would accomplish more.

The seven-hour drive from Chicago to Canton the next day was filled with a disturbing recollection of the peculiar behaviors Dick had exhibited over the last few years. He took pride in saving money on motel rooms by sleeping in his truck in Walmart parking lots under the security lights. His grooming habits up north had declined to where Carole didn't even want him in the house because of his body odor. Social contact was limited to dinners with us, though only after Carole insisted he shower. The rare interaction with neighbors who happened along the road—and of course his "conversations" with Cinder—filled out his dance card.

I reflected on the comments John Walsh, Dick's former college roommate, had made about Dick's behavior during a 2006 trip to East Lansing for the annual Michigan State University Football Players Association golf outing. For years, I had encouraged Dick to attend, but he never showed interest. I think John's verbal encouragement—and his willingness to pay for a shared room—helped Dick over the hurdle. The weather gods didn't cooperate, however, and the April outing was snowed out, which allowed Dick and John to spend Friday together.

John told me Dick talked nonstop about his accomplishments and personal successes:

> *Dick talked about his ski home in New York and a situation where his neighbor was doing a project all wrong. He told me he stood watching, not saying anything until the neighbor asked what he wanted. Dick told him he could do it better and that the neighbor's approach was backward. "How much would it cost to do it your way?" the neighbor asked. "Nothing," Dick said. "I'll do it for free just to help out." In three quarters of an hour, Dick was done, and the guy acknowledged that his approach was good. Dick said, "I know. I'm good. Glad I could help."*

While this may seem like being a "good neighbor," John could tell that Dick's whole motive was the recognition of being better than the man he helped.

It wasn't until Saturday after breakfast that Dick finally showed interest in hearing about John and his life. John was open with his successes as a president and CEO of a privately held manufacturing company and his involvement in the venture capital business. John continued by describing an assignment in Wisconsin where the business had less than one week's worth of cash flow and John was able to keep them in operation for a year.

Dick's response was, "You fucked up," using uncharacteristic language.

John also told Dick about a detached retina issue and operation, along with prostate cancer challenges. Dick showed no empathy, no personal connection, no validation of John's situations. He was just a dark shadow avoiding someone sharing a disappointment.

None of our conversation that weekend made sense. I remember Dick as someone with high standards, for sure. Not a complainer. Good at time management, and a good role model—particularly for me. Sure, he was a perfectionist with a kind of "tsk, tsk" admonishment for those who didn't get it. But he was always friendly and helpful. He just needed to loosen up, that's all.

One comment that Dick made, in particular, struck me as odd, as it was all about the hard-copy tax records being burned in the fire and no backup support for IRS audits. All I could remember was the color-coordinated clothes laid out and the completely organized desk in college. The Dick I knew would have never let that happen.

Ken Bankey, another quarterback on the Michigan State team in the early '60s and roommate of Dick's, also related similar feelings as John's, remembering Dick as "organized, up and at 'em in the morning, very serious about studies, but needed to expand his fun side." Ken stood up for Dick in his marriage with Diane but had little contact with Dick after the MSU days.

The flurry created by these thoughts occupied my drive without resolution. To compare and contrast "then" and "now" was remarkable.

I had never been to Dick and Paula's Lawndale home. The relevance of its location—backing up to Canton's most exclusive community, Hills and Dales—did not go unnoticed, though. In reality, their home might as well have been a hundred miles away from Hills and Dales. At one time, this ranch home, nicely positioned on a beautiful hardwood-treed lot, must have been very nice. But now the lack of yard maintenance and exterior home care told an economic story common to northeast Ohio.

Paula was surprised when she answered the call of the doorbell. For that matter, I was surprised she had returned from Hilton Head.

"Jim, what are you doing here? You should have said you were coming."

"I was on the phone with Dick yesterday, and quite frankly, I was concerned. So I decided to visit firsthand."

"Did you drive from Chicago?" she asked.

"Yes. I got an early start."

"Well, now that you're here, c'mon in. It's a bit of a mess, as we're having some work done."

"A bit of a mess" was a gross understatement, and they weren't "having some work done." It was filthy. I could see what Patty meant. From the foyer to the living room, dining room, and kitchen were card tables and counters laden with paperwork, mail, uneaten food on plates, wrappers, and every form of trash conceivable. Expensive wall hangings and collectibles from their big home were sitting against the wall as if in a poorly organized warehouse. Nothing had been dusted in a long time, if ever.

Paula was dressed fashionably, but Dick looked the part of a street bum. After a while, Dick finally noticed I was there, even though Paula and I had walked by him several times while he watched TV in his La-Z-Boy. He may have been napping. More mail—opened and unopened—was in disarray on the end tables flanking his chair.

"Hi, Dick," I said, specifically avoiding the use of "Richard."

He tried to get up but couldn't, clearly struggling with balance. "Hey," he said in a slurred, vague recognition of me. "What are you doing here?"

"After talking to Patty and Mike yesterday, it sounded like you might need some more help. Are you trying to get the place ready to sell?"

"Nothing's selling around here. And the bank's putting pressure on us."

"What's going on, Paula?" I said, directing my physical attention toward her.

"Things aren't going well. The house is in trouble with the bank, and Dick isn't making payments."

Quite a comment, I thought, *from a woman who just returned from a one-week vacation with friends at the Hilton Head time-share.*

"He won't let me near the finances and shuts me out when I try to get involved."

"Dick, you trust me, don't you?" I said, turning back to Dick.

"Yes," he said, nodding in a truncated response. His lack of interaction in dialogue was more noticeable, as if he struggled to hold on to multiple sets of thoughts.

"Let's talk about your situation, but I need you to be completely open with me about your money position . . . okay?"

"Okay." His posture and tone were in complete submission as we moved to the kitchen table, where we could talk.

Before we sat down, I had imagined the worst-case scenario was a severe cash flow issue. But I was wrong—it was much worse.

The first thing I looked at was an out-of-date net worth statement from the '90s valuing Dick's estate at over $12 million. He was very proud of it and seemed to hold on to it as if it were still valid. Good news, until you peeled the onion back. The Great Recession and 9/11 weren't good for business, as everyone knows. But in northeast Ohio, the heart of the Rust Belt, the pain many felt was huge. And Dick had become a poster child for wealthy men whose investment strategies were solely wrapped up in real estate in one of the worst markets in the United States.

With one exception, every piece of business property—including buildings in Canton, Akron, and Mansfield—were either in foreclosure or had significant liens from creditors: the county, the state, and/or the IRS. Most frequently the *and* in the *and/or* was operative. With dormant buildings, aging infrastructure, and no money for maintenance, the Akron and Canton properties were in the condemnation process. The only exception to this disaster was that a second home in Ellicottville, New York, was owned outright and clean from obligations.

Their personal finances were no better. There was a foreclosure on their Lawndale home, property tax liens, plus State of Ohio and IRS income tax liens. Boats had been seized in Florida, and property in Arizona had been foreclosed upon as well. Their sole source of income was a tenuous rent payment of $3,000 per month from a Mid-States property in Mansfield. It looked as if the lessee was about to contest that rent, limiting payment to $1,500 per month.

As if I weren't shocked enough, some of their time-shares had been foreclosed upon, and all were in arrears on maintenance payments. Credit cards had been revoked, and the remaining active Citibank card, shared by he and Paula, had a $12,843 balance. Along with Paula using this card for various personal and household purchases, Dick had been making gimmick purchases on the late-night QVC network.

It was beyond any understanding how Dick's decision-making had become so bad, for so many years, on so many levels. The Dick we used to know and respect had "left the house." I didn't know where to start.

Over the next two hours, I also found out Dick had not been signed up for Social Security or Medicare, with corresponding stacks of unpaid medical bills. Paula informed me that her Social Security income was for *her* to live on.

I was pissed. "Paula, Dick's got obvious medical needs with no means to pay for them!"

Besides the noticeable issues of cognitive decline that required a series of psychiatric tests, Dick needed dentistry work, physical exams for heart irregularities, and a general physical exam. They were all long overdue. The problem was that he had not paid doctors for previous visits, so he was persona non grata. Without Medicare, he was in a catch-22 scenario.

"He wouldn't let me help," Paula replied.

"That's not right, Paula. It's obvious he can't help himself."

How could you treat your spouse that way? I thought.

* * *

It was an eye-opening day, and I challenged everything going on. I didn't want to end on a sour note, though, so I decided we should have a good meal together.

"Is there a restaurant that's a favorite of Dick's?" I asked Paula.

As it turned out, there was—Baker's, a family steak restaurant on the south side of town. The place was crowded and noisy, but the steaks were excellent. Dick's focus was on the food, not the interaction. In his defense, it was hard to hear. But I couldn't help noticing, once again, the parkinsonian similarity to our mom's behavior around food—guarded and single-minded, very purposeful.

When we got up to leave, Dick stood and began putting on his ski jacket. Paula and I had already left for the door, but when I turned around, I saw Dick still standing at the table in the middle of the crowded restaurant, fiddling with the zipper, struggling to get it started.

I walked over. "Can I help?"

"No." His expression was determined, as if to say, *Why would you ask to help? I'm just zipping my jacket.*

He insisted on standing at the table, attempting to start the zipper, even though he was in the way of the servers trying to clean up. It was uncomfortable as I watched him struggle—probably five minutes. The odd part to me was that he didn't consider his actions out of place, just determined.

It reminded me of a situation Patty had related about a recent visit at her home in Newtown, Pennsylvania. Like all dads, he wanted to help, so he offered to assemble and install a new half-screen-and-half-window front door. Seven hours later, the door was finally hung.

CHAPTER 16

* * *

Identifying the problems was as much as I could accomplish on that trip, although letting Dick know help was available was likely beneficial, as well. I planned to return the next week, when Patty could be there also. Before I left, I gave Paula a list of things to be done before my return. One was to create an inventory of the valuable joint assets and art objects that could be sold, with their approximate values and authentication documentation. She wasn't very happy.

On my way home, I drove by our old home at Lake Cable, a community in North Canton where many of our family memories were formed. Like most people, I need that occasional physical connection to reinforce my emotional stability. From there, I was traveling across Portage Road toward US Route 21 when the enormity of the events erupted. I pulled to the side of the road—traffic was light. The pit of my stomach was in an uproar of frustration, anger, and sorrow. I needed a minute to clear my emotions and reflect.

How could this happen? It was becoming an all-too-frequent thought.

I had admired and loved Dick my entire life. For this to take place was an insult so deep, I knew he would never recover.

Regardless of his current mental condition or past personal responsibilities, this torture he was saddled with had to end. I had to help make it come to an end.

CHAPTER 17

We were exposed to the piles of
unfulfilled obligations hidden in the closet:
bills, contracts, tax liens, and more.

The family wagons were circled. Patty went into full gear helping her dad initiate a divorce with Paula. It was clear to us that Paula's interests lay only with what she could still get out of "Richard." She was otherwise absent from his life both emotionally and physically. Before heading out on her vacations, she had a habit of filling a bowl with batches of food that would last Dick several days—the way you would feed a pet during an extended absence. That probably says it all. It's hard to imagine such mistreatment and exploitation of someone you claim to love. Dick was left to fend for himself in a sea of depression.

The valuable joint assets and artwork she promised to document were never seen again. And while Paula's vacations and spending continued, Dick led a very fragile and frugal lifestyle, trying to make ends meet.

Dick needed the family's support in order to muster the courage to go through the divorce. Dick relayed to me that he and Paula had once discussed how a friend's husband had "walked out" on her. Paula indicated to Dick that if such a thing ever happened to her, she would have Gary, her son, "take care of things."

"Gary is in the concrete business and knows how to handle paybacks," Dick told me.

Even if Paula had been exaggerating or joking, which is possible, I know Dick viewed this as a threat of bodily harm. Considering his judgment issues and diminished level of reasoning, he may have been living in fear.

Other than a surface show of emotion in a phone call with me at a later date, Paula didn't contest the divorce. She was out of the picture, at least for the time being. It was simple: when the cupboard was bare, she left.

* * *

Over the next two years or so, Patty, Mike, and I focused on the goal of eliminating the complexities Dick faced in order to make an easier life for him to enjoy.

Once Patty got involved, it took only a few months to sort things out with Medicare and Social Security. Setting up Social Security opened the door to paying the unpaid medical bills and getting the treatment he needed. Even if Dick's Social Security income was only $1,800 per month, it was something.

And we finally found the last piles of hidden, unfulfilled obligations—bills, contracts, tax liens, and more. We had known they existed somewhere. *He must have been terribly shamed,* I thought. Once we were able to peek through his veil of confusion, we recognized Dick's inability to comprehend the disease that had plagued him for years.

We had many unusual encounters in our attempts to unravel Dick's "ball of twine" and create cash for him to live on. The people involved in these encounters ran the gamut from loyal and generous to cruel and despicable.

Cutler Real Estate—through the efforts of Jim Bray, president, and Bill Rearick, agent—demonstrated their friendship to Dick by pitching in to sell some of the land he held. Jim was a friend from MSU, and Bill had represented Dick on real estate transactions in the past. Jim, Bill, and I worked on one property at a time, dealing with depressed values and peeling back the inevitable contingency components to each sale involving liens of all sorts.

Many of the twenty-six time-share weeks were ultimately lost to foreclosure, voluntary or otherwise. Paula kept Hilton Head as part of the divorce settlement. Only one of the time-shares sold, netting $4,000 to $5,000 after liens and expenses. The Stark County properties were also particularly hard to sell, as a six-figure summary lien was in place for all properties held. Dick wouldn't see any money until the lien was satisfied.

The business properties in Canton and Akron were especially challenging. We found out that in Dick's desperation and illusion that he was still running his business, he had made an undisclosed "business relationship" with an Akron businessman. The agreement allowed this man to take all of Dick's remaining inventory of lift trucks, skid-steer loaders, and parts—valued at approximately $100,000—with the intent to ship and sell it overseas in Lebanon. Additionally, salvage people stripped the Canton building of valuable copper wiring under this person's direction. Dick never saw a dime.

Underlying much of the issue was Dick's inability to

articulate his words and think on his feet in dealings such as this. Instead, he got frustrated and just let the other person take control of the discussion, much like how Paula took control of his life. That may have been the case with this arrangement. The man was a hustler and had no problems taking advantage of an obviously diminished person. He will have to account for himself in another life.

The contract Dick had prepared and signed, along with Paula as dower, showed no indication of clear business thinking and/or strategy. "Richard, this contract doesn't make sense," Paula had said, objecting strenuously. But her objections were ignored; according to her, she was coerced into signing. This was a pattern as we uncovered Dick's business dealings—it seemed Dick fashioned himself a lawyer and did his own contracts.

We had little recourse. Although the contract was nonsense, it didn't restrict this man's actions, which precluded filing a police report. I investigated the possibility of making a claim of elder abuse with the State of Ohio. But they couldn't offer support without our hiring an attorney, as Dick "owned too much property." We asked Dick to file criminal charges against the businessman, but he wouldn't do it. We had to let it go.

Another challenge was the business property in Mansfield. It was the only source of income—but it was spiraling out of control. The part owner of the towing business leasing the property had already bullied Dick into a temporary agreement of $1,500 per month because of some disagreements regarding building deficiencies. Once again, the contract was vague.

Then the lessee tried to take advantage of Dick and sabotage us at every opportunity, particularly in our efforts to sell the property. This situation got personal, as I was handling the sale myself. We valued the property at about $120,000, but he made a ridiculous lowball offer I would not entertain. At that point, the lessee attempted to discourage every interested party by telling them it wasn't worth anywhere near our asking price. He was rude, unprofessional, and completely unsympathetic to our situation.

The silver lining came when I uncovered a dispute regarding an underground water repair project shared with the business owner next door. Dick had never paid a plumbing bill worth over $30,000. I called Dave Grabowsky, president of Standard Plumbing and Heating, headquartered in Canton. It was a tough introduction, as the debt was more than a year overdue. After explaining Dick's situation, I asked if they might have interest in the building as a branch office, and if so, they could take the $30,000 off the list price. He said they had been looking for a new location and asked what I proposed.

Forgoing the details, I can say Dave was a breath of fresh air—a Rotarian, I soon discovered, as I was. With the motto "To be fair to all concerned," I knew we could work together, and we did. To this day, I hold Dave in great respect. It's not a surprise that the business his father founded is one of the two oldest in Canton (the other being Belden Brick). Honesty and integrity are never out of style.

* * *

As we sorted through the financial mess, I began to wonder if we were missing something. I quickly realized a portfolio completely made up of real estate, with its inherent liquidity challenges, is not the way to prepare for retirement. Yet Dick had no reserve of cash or securities—none we could find, at least.

Dick had always been very secretive about his money, so I couldn't rule anything out. With all those poor decisions in the business, perhaps Dick had attempted to cover up mistakes—or worse, cover up fraud—by hiding money. If this were the situation, there had to be cash somewhere, I reasoned.

I even recalled a bizarre discovery at our Leech Lake property a few years earlier, where Dick had stashed a few household items from our inheritance under a makeshift tent in the middle of the forest. I uncovered the stash in the spring—after everything had been destroyed by the winter. It was hard to find the logic of his actions, but it was startling evidence that he would go to extremes to keep his affairs private.

"Dick, level with me," I said one afternoon. "Are there any other accounts where you might have cash? What about offshore accounts, Dick? You know, places where you could keep your money tax-free."

"Why would I do that?" he replied.

"I don't know why, but I do know that people use those accounts."

He didn't say anything. It's possible he was just avoiding the ugly implication of fraud and didn't want to dignify my question with an answer. Or maybe he was unable to face the tangled mess of incompetent decisions. I never did get the clear answer I was looking for.

Through it all, though, I did see a growing sense of relief in his demeanor. He knew he could place his trust in me, although at times I could visibly see the diminished pride and embarrassment in his expression.

* * *

Dick told me privately that he didn't want to be seen as a deadbeat in the community, so we worked hard to accomplish that. In the end, all of his debts were cleared. Slowly, the sale of the land helped satisfy the various obligations as well as provided some cash for his inevitable long-term-care needs.

Dick appointed Patty power of attorney (POA). Carole and I felt safe in relying on her judgment, with Mike's input, as to how the money should be allocated. Dick challenged her, every step of the way, on nitpicky items, so I often found myself playing the role of arbiter. He knew if I sided with Mike and Patty, there was a strong likelihood theirs was the correct approach. I tried to be fair and, at times, took his side too.

Not a pretty time for anyone, but it was over. The basics were in place to provide for Dick financially. More importantly, Paula was gone, and Mike and Patty were in charge. They loved their father and would do anything to improve the quality of his life.

SECTION IV

CTE CLOSING MOMENTS— YOUR BRAIN IS BEYOND REPAIR

CHAPTER 18

None of the moves to maintain
Dick's independence worked—
New York, Pennsylvania, or Indiana.

With the Lawndale property lost via foreclosure, Dick's options to stay in Canton were limited. His emotional connection to our "home turf" would never change—his self-image had been forged there. Consequently, moving from Ohio to New York seemed more like an escape than a voluntary change of address.

The silver lining was that the home in Ellicottville had always been a favorite winter ski getaway for Dick and Paula, but 2008 was the height of turmoil on all fronts. The Ellicottville home was the only bastion, in that it was encumbrance-free. As such, Dick was able to remove some equity, take out a reverse mortgage, and create some badly needed cash flow in order to make this his permanent residence.

Mike moved Dick's possessions with a truck in May. Patty was on the New York end of things to help.

"I can't believe these clothes," she said to Mike upon arrival. "It looks like thirty years of stuff. Some of it smells from being worn and not laundered. It's disgusting."

Both were embarrassed by the closed-loop mentality defining their dad's life. They held back further judgment and continued with the task at hand.

With the move and the divorce nearing finality, Dick finally had some breathing room. Paula was being moved out of the picture. Despite the emotional stress of leaving Canton, Dick seemed optimistic about the move and the stabilization of his financial condition.

But true to form, trouble wasn't far behind. Bobbie Jean saw Dick's move as an opportunity to escape her living conditions in the projects in Akron. She had managed to keep her claws in Dick ever since their affair began while he was married to Paula. Several years earlier, Dick had paid for her move from Arizona back to Ohio and subsidized her apartment rental. It was all for the availability of sex— which, according to Dick, Paula had been withholding for some time and was one basis point for the divorce. Dick just didn't seem able to see the faulty logic. So with Dick moving to Ellicottville, BJ took a bus in an attempt to finally have him all to herself.

Paula had conveniently planned a visit to the Hilton Head time-share during Dick's move. That's why her unexpected arrival in Ellicottville was a surprise no one saw coming. She had come to make a last attempt to get Dick to call off the divorce. All hell broke loose when Paula discovered BJ.

Patty had her hands full with these two hustlers under the same roof. Paula attempted to reestablish marital relations that night to get what she wanted from Dick. But Patty was well prepared and cut her off at the pass. She knew Paula's effort at reconciliation was a sham.

CHAPTER 18

"Dad, you're not going to let Paula sleep in your bedroom tonight. It will undo everything."

The next day, Paula gathered her snowmen art collection of over a hundred pieces and left. BJ left shortly thereafter, though her relationship with Dick would continue. At least for one day, Patty had miraculously defended her father.

Dick settled in for a while, making connections with neighbors. One lady he met was Donna, a dental hygienist where Dick was receiving services. Donna cared for her kids and grandkids, all living in her house. She was single— or at least living in a single-parent situation—and took an interest in Dick. She brought him soup and prepared food. Dick, of course, loved the attention and encouraged the relationship. He seemed to have a skill in attracting women who would care for him, and Donna was no different.

Over time, however, we learned it was always about his wealth, which he believed still existed. Spinning scenarios where his money would become part of the relationship was attractive to a certain type of woman. Donna was more stable than the others, though, and for a while, her interest in Dick was supportive.

For the first time in years, Dick felt at home. He seemed to actually improve—taking walks with Cinder, meeting other neighbors, and gaining some confidence.

* * *

But early the next year, a bizarre set of circumstances showed a new depth in Dick's decline. Patty called Dick to arrange a visit at his home, but Bobbie Jean was there at the time. Patty wanted to spend time with her dad, so Bobbie Jean's presence was not an option. Dick drove Bobbie Jean back to Akron, then agreed to pick up Patty at the Pittsburgh airport to make the reminder of the trip back to Ellicottville together.

All the Proebstle brothers grew up knowing geography, maps, and directions; getting lost was extremely unusual. Yet Dick became so disoriented—in daylight, no less—at the I-80–I-76 interchange west of Youngstown, Ohio, that he had to exit the expressway to seek help at a gas station and food market. He thought he was speaking normally, but the merchant couldn't understand him. Police were called, and Dick was taken to a local minister's house until things could be sorted out. It was obvious he wasn't able to continue on his own.

The minister and his wife fed Dick and were ultimately able to connect with Patty to arrange a hand-off of her dad. Patty rented a car at the airport and drove to Youngstown. Not trusting that Dick could drive, the minister and his wife generously caravanned with Patty and Dick back to the airport, so Patty could return the rental and continue their way to Ellicottville with Dick's car. Patty could not thank them enough for saving the day. Patty and Dick arrived late, completely exhausted, and went immediately to bed.

The next day, Dick reacted as if nothing happened or was wrong—detached and in denial. But the situation must have worked its way into his thinking. He told Patty later, "I'm starting to change. I won't be here in five years," he said. "My thinking isn't clear, and I can't remember like I used to."

This shocked Patty, as it was Dick's first acknowledgment that something was wrong. *Pretty amazing,* she thought, *considering all the disasters up to this point.*

For the first time, Dick also admitted confusion about the Richard J. Proebstle Trust, his vehicle to keep assets from Paula's reach. Patty was named cotrustee in the 2006 modification with Jim Bright, the attorney who authored the trust. Patty needed to get more involved with the trust, but Jim was reluctant to help. As it turned out, the trail of Dick's unpaid bills included Jim, which seemed to be the root cause. Once satisfied, Jim's help was forthcoming. Despite the pattern of Dick's financial irresponsibility and the inevitable shadow of embarrassment, Patty soldiered on, eliminating one problem after another.

Shortly thereafter, Patty made an emergency return visit to Ellicottville. Dick had passed out at a local community event. Upon coming to, he refused help. All he said was, "Take me home." Neighbors also told Patty that Dick had been getting lost on walks. One neighbor related that Dick had asked, "Where do I live?"

During that visit, Patty noticed continued confusion. She would find her dad just standing in a room with no sense of purpose. He slept all the time on his recliner, his body twisting and contorting in a very odd manner, almost causing him to fall out of his chair. He couldn't make meals. His frozen, glassy look became more persistent, and he constantly rubbed his fingers together with a hungover or drugged look.

She purchased a Life Alert system for him, and it served its purpose when he had a heart attack shortly after. He was successfully fitted with a pacemaker, but under no circumstances would the doctors release him under his own recognizance.

* * *

I don't know if the move to Ellicottville served a lasting emotional purpose for Dick or not. Regardless, he was upset about having to leave and move in with Patty in Newtown, Pennsylvania, in October 2009. He had enjoyed his brief encounter with independence, but moving in with Patty seemed to be the best option. Donna's surprising proposal for Dick to move in with her and her flock of kids was rejected as completely unmanageable from any variety of viewpoints.

The day of the move, Dick threw a fit when Patty beat him to the driver's seat of the loaded van. "You don't know how to drive this big truck," he told her.

"Remember when I drove the dump truck to get twelve yards of mulch when I was sixteen? I did okay."

He nodded a begrudging agreement.

"Besides, you're not really fit to drive long distances, Dad. Why don't you help navigate?"

He wasn't happy, but he agreed.

Patty quickly learned that taking care of Dick required changes in her life. He couldn't use stairs, had toileting issues, faced meal-preparation challenges, and more. Supervising Dick was like supervising a preschooler. The one thing he did like was helping outside with lawn and gardening, just as he had helped Carole and me in 1982 with the landscaping project. It was in his DNA.

Patty made arrangements with her employer, American Express, to alter her work schedule, limiting out-of-town travel and overnights. She was gone, however, for hours at a time, making sales calls with clients in New York City. During those periods, Dick racked up hours and expenses on the cell phone talking with the notorious BJ. She was like a bad penny.

Despite Patty's efforts to make things work, however, it was apparent that Dick needed more than she could provide. Dick aggressively shut down any discussion of assisted living. Patty, Mike, and I talked things out and agreed that Mike's situation in Warsaw, Indiana, was much more conducive, so one more move was planned.

I actually think Dick thought the moves were exciting, but they were hell on Patty and Mike. So the plan was for Patty and her dad to visit Ellicottville over Christmas on the way to Indiana. Mike loaded the same-sized truck he had unloaded three months previously; this time, it was in the middle of a blizzard. Dick moved in with Mike right around New Year's Day 2010.

Everyone was happy. The situation was ideal. Mike and Dick moved into a new rental home, set up perfectly for Dick's situation—a separate main-floor suite with a living room, bedroom, and bathroom. The house was on a small bay of a lake, not dissimilar to our home growing up on Lake Cable in North Canton. The property allowed room to enjoy the outdoors.

Dick had lost his driving privileges—the by-product of his heart attack and growing confusion with directions. The stress of multiple moves had been of no help in this regard, either. Dick accepted the situation but missed driving. As an alternative, he briefly enjoyed driving his John Deere Gator down the long driveway adjacent to their property. But even that didn't last. Because of Dick's rapidly declining motor skills, Mike had to disable the Gator for fear of an accident.

Even without the Gator, Dick really enjoyed the simple pleasure of walking the long driveway, picking branches off the entryway to the neighbor's home. During our first visit that spring, he told me, "No one's ever had the branches picked up like this before. I just flick them to the side with my rake." His world had gone from small to microscopic. The brain shrinkage from CTE must have been accelerating, but we still were in the dark that his dementia had a name.

I was happy he was taking pride in his efforts, though. Dick's social interaction was lacking, so Carole, Mike, and I took him to downtown Warsaw to see if we could get him oriented. Mike wasn't sure this would work, but we thought maybe the library, senior center, and movie theater might have activities that would interest him. Warsaw's downtown area is small, and the public transportation system was designed for seniors with limited skills.

"What do you think, Dick?" I asked while we walked the main square.

He shrugged. "I don't know."

"What do you mean?"

"It's not for me," he said. He was honestly trying to be enthused, but it just wasn't happening.

"Let's check out the library and see what they have," I offered, not letting his first reaction set the tone.

The facilities were excellent, including several rooms with couches and chairs for adult reading. The head librarian took interest in our questions and also tried to engage Dick with brochures of the seniors' programs. But the library option just wasn't happening for Dick either.

On the sidewalk outside, I fell back a few steps to talk with Carole. "I think the problem is that Dick doesn't relate to being old or being in a setting dominated by older people. He just doesn't want to go there."

"Do you think *you* would?" she replied.

"You're right. Maybe it's a problem I'll have too. I mean, it's not like getting old and having limited capacities is anyone's goal. But still, I think social stimulation is important."

Looking back, I now recognize that Dick, in his need for independence, had become progressively isolated in his day-to-day activities. His property in Massillon, the Minnesota property, and his business properties had all led him to very private, hands-on, outdoor physical activities. The idea of going downtown and sitting in a library to read a newspaper wasn't Dick. He needed to be relevant on his terms. He was a quarterback, in charge of making things happen. But those options were hard to find in his condition.

Once again, Dick isolated himself. Mike made a big effort to include his girlfriend in activities around the house to engage Dick. For a while, Mike's girls, Erin and Ellie, enjoyed frequent visits and weekend stay-overs while he had custody. But Dick quickly became agitated and irritable with their rambunctious play. He always seemed to "behave," however, when Carole and I visited, then he'd return to a state of discontent once we left.

The move to Warsaw started on such a positive note, but then it devolved quickly into a lack of cooperation on Dick's part. It became a "Mike do this, Mike do that" scenario, with no appreciation for the efforts being made. In Dick's delusion, Mike was the son who never measured up. Dick's continual verbal abuse was wearing thin. It was frustrating for Mike, as he had a full-time job as well. He was a contract production engineer with Zimmer, the artificial knee company. He had no medical benefits and couldn't afford to mess up.

Also eroding any positive outcome of the living

arrangement was the costly distraction of Dick's ongoing cell phone conversations with BJ, and now Bridget, Paula's granddaughter. "Mike and Patty are taking advantage of you and robbing you blind," both BJ and Bridget were reported saying to Dick. The nonstop "ain't it awful treatment" conversations had Dick believing he was still capable of doing anything he wanted. It was what he wanted to hear. They put him in a constant mental state of "get me out of here." It's hard to imagine how these two women could continue to intervene, each with her own selfish agenda to take care of Dick herself. We knew these conversations were harmful to Dick, but we didn't feel it was right to restrict his cell phone use either—it was a challenging dilemma.

Then came the call from Mike. "Uncle Jim, you're not going to believe this one."

I had gotten used to calls like this. "What's this about?"

"Dad has hired a local lawyer to void Patty's power of attorney. He's also made arrangements with the U-Haul dealer to rent a truck to move to Ohio. The plan is for the lawyer to pick Dick up and take him to the U-Haul center while I'm at work."

"*What*?" This was one for the ages. "How did you find this out?"

"The call came to the house yesterday. I answered. The U-Haul company wanted to verify the pickup date. What do I do now?"

After getting names and contact numbers, I told Mike I would get back to him. My first call was to the U-Haul company.

After introducing myself and being connected to the manager, I said, "I'm calling on behalf of my brother Dick Proebstle. I understand he has a reservation for one of your trucks."

"Yes, that's right—one of our box trucks."

I actually smiled, knowing of Dick's comfort over the years with box trucks.

"Have you met Dick or just talked over the phone?"

"He was driven here by another man—his lawyer, I believe. Arrangements have been made for the attorney to pick the truck up."

"Well, there are a few complications," I said. "My brother has dementia and has a revoked driver's license. He can appear put-together at times, and then not so much at other times."

Silence on the other end.

"It's a long story," I continued, "but he won't be able to complete his obligation for the rental. Did he make a deposit on his credit card?"

"We have a number but haven't charged anything yet."

"Thank you, and please don't," I said. "The situation is a little confusing."

"I understand," the manager said in a cooperative and sympathetic voice. "How about the lawyer?"

"I'll call him right away and clear things up. Thank you, and have a good day."

I was on to my next call.

"Law offices," said a female voice. It's always been my experience that this sort of generic phone reception is reserved for lawyers using an answering service to front as a receptionist. I announced my interest in speaking to Dick's attorney.

"Please hold for a minute."

After a brief hold, the attorney announced himself.

"We've not met, but my name is Jim Proebstle. I'm

calling on behalf of my brother Dick Proebstle and his son, Mike Proebstle. I understand you plan to pick my brother up and transport him to the U-Haul center in a few days. Is that right?"

"Well, yes, I do, but I don't see how it's a matter of concern to you," he answered in his best lawyer tone.

"As of now, I'm making it my business. And if you value your license to practice law in the state of Indiana, you'll listen very closely." I brought him up to speed on the bigger picture, then asked, "Do you still feel it's wise to act on Dick's behalf in assisting him in renting a truck without a valid license and driving it to another state?"

"No, I don't," was the sheepish reply.

"Good, because the rental contract has already been canceled. Thank you. Do we also need to talk about your efforts to revoke his daughter's power of attorney?"

"No. I understand," was the sheepish reply once again.

I hung up. I was furious about how stupid people could be. I realized Dick could still be persuasive in his own way, but I couldn't for the life of me figure how low on the attorney totem pole this guy must have been to charge hourly rates for services like this.

* * *

At the cabin in Minnesota that summer, I heard from one of Dick's Central Catholic High School classmates. He was planning to pick Dick up at Mike's house on his way from Chicago so Dick could attend their fiftieth high school reunion in Canton. The friend had just visited Dick in the previous months and was amazed about how "well" Dick was doing.

CHAPTER 18

By now, I had become a little suspicious of these spontaneous interventions. I wondered if Dick had solicited this high school friend in yet another attempt to move back to Ohio. But that suspicion was mitigated when I learned that Mike Fay and Jane (Matthews) Steiner, trustworthy friends of Dick and the family, would also be at the reunion. They understood Dick's instability and rapid decline and had everyone's best interests at heart.

I think I was getting defensive of outside questioning about Dick's care. As a team caring for Dick, we had learned there were highs and lows to the dementia. The visits and attention from outsiders naturally stimulated a high. This high school friend had seen Dick during one of his highs, when Dick inevitably claimed that his relatives, including me, were stealing from him. Like the U-Haul scenario and POA revocation attempt, these challenges were relatively easy to handle but nonetheless hurtful.

Dick could sway outsiders. "They've taken all my money," "they're keeping me here against my will," or some paranoia to that effect was the common plea. What Dick couldn't grasp was that Patty, Mike, and I weren't the "they." Dick was very vulnerable to hustlers, and in reality, "they" had already taken all his money. We were the ones desperately trying to salvage what was left.

"I'm doing everything I can," Mike said to me on many occasions. And he was. With Dick's history of treating them like second-class citizens over the years, Mike and Patty finally learned to accept that the anger, paranoia, and claims of mistreatment were symptoms of his condition. They learned not to take things personally as best as possible. But it was hard. It always hurt when others questioned Mike and Patty's efforts, based on a limited exposure

191

framed by Dick's distorted perspective.

In truth, I think it was confusing for others, such as this high school friend, to have the 24-7 perspective: to see the Dick who was completely dependent, the Dick whose volatile outrages had forced Mike to stop taking his two girls to visit their grandpa, the Dick who had few skills left to understand his life. When friends saw Dick in this debilitated state, trying to reclaim a life he didn't realize was beyond his grasp, I learned to accept that it made them, in fact, anxious. They were just reacting, as we all do, to some inner hope for a different future for Dick—and maybe themselves.

The fiftieth reunion escapade became another disappointing example of decline. Dick had secretly arranged for BJ to meet him at the motel room in Canton, which they didn't leave for most of the reunion. I'm sure she agreed to meet him with the hopes of restarting the cash machine.

When Dick's friends who were "looking out for him" came to the motel to pick him up for the reunion dinner, they were greeted by this partially dressed "guest" making excuses that Dick was unavailable.

"Tell them to go away!" Dick yelled in the background.

Dick's friends shrugged, laughed like teenagers, and let Dick humiliate himself as the rumor of his behavior spread through the evening function. This was the dinner where his classmates had arranged for a letter to be presented to Dick from our former coach, John McVay, attesting to Dick's prowess and contribution to Central as a student athlete.

The next day, Dick attended the group function but had difficulty getting himself out of his chair to join the buffet line. Coupled with his imbalance and inability to serve himself, it was quite noticeable. His friends were eager to help him that morning.

It seems the need for physical support is easy to recognize, yet the need for mental and psychological help is hard to come by. It's like the football injuries of old: the player with the broken bone is treated with care, while the player with the concussion never leaves the field or returns to play in short order. Dick's friends were sympathetic to his physical difficulties yet didn't realize Dick had reached new lows for disinhibitive behaviors, which are inappropriate actions that would normally be filtered out.

Whether well-meaning or manipulative, outsiders had little awareness that their actions and provocations kept Dick in a state of turmoil and displayed complete disrespect for Mike and Patty.

CHAPTER 19

"Why don't we just let him sleep?
I'll have the security officer give him
a blanket and some bottled water . . ."

One of my last and most frustrating remembrances of my dad's death in '88 was the inability to create a final visit to our cabin on Leech Lake. My father spent a segment of his youth growing up in Cass Lake, Minnesota, one lake north of Leech Lake. His second-grade picture is in Lyle's Logging Camp, the local museum. I still show our guests the empty lot on the corner of Fourth and Elm in Cass Lake, where the home he lived in from 1915 to 1925 once stood. Today the town is a run-down Ojibwe Indian community in much need of a face-lift, but it's special to us.

In my dad's case, we waited too long. The aggressive progress of his pancreatic cancer prevented that last trip to the cabin. It prevented his final connection to the land that coursed through his blood for a lifetime. The trip would have provided an undeclared reconciliation for all those thoughts and emotions playing in the background of his life.

Carole, Mike, Patty, and I weren't about to let what happened to Dad happen to Dick. Dick's dementia and growing depression continued in a shocking, rapid decline the summer of 2010. Postponement wasn't an option.

* * *

While Carole and I were ready for Dick's arrival in Minnesota, it was up to Mike to make the trip happen.

Amazingly, Dick was still of the mind-set that there was little wrong with him and much to be desired in his living arrangement. Mike was still struggling with a father whose dark judgment made the living arrangement tense and unfulfilling for both of them. They each knew a break was needed.

Mike saw that the duffel bag was still empty on his dad's bed. "Dad, you've got to get packed. Your flight to Uncle Jim and Aunt Carole's leaves in three hours."

"Stop telling me what to do!" The combative tone had become the norm.

"Can I help? I mean, you may need some things they don't have." Mike was referring to the Depends that Dick was in denial about.

"No!"

Dick's desire to make the trip, however, ultimately greased the wheels for some level of cooperation. Mike accepted the reality that Dick's preparation would be less than perfect if they were to make the flight on time.

"Who's this?" Dick said with a hostile attitude as Mike introduced him to the airline personnel charged with ensuring his successful transit.

"They're going to make sure you connect with your flight to Bemidji at Minneapolis–Saint Paul. No big thing."

We had enlisted some help from the staff, as we were all concerned that the only connecting flight to Bemidji, a town west of Leech Lake, was also the last one of the day.

"You think I can't do anything. I was flying into Minneapolis–Saint Paul before you were born." Dick's demeanor showed disgust with Mike's interference. His cooperation with the attendant during the flight was at a bare minimum.

Murphy's Law was at work that day. The flight arrived too late for Dick, or his bags, to make the connection. He would have to stay at a local hotel the airline provided for him. He was confused with what to do about his luggage, as he thought it had been checked through to Bemidji. Consequently, he never claimed it. He was wearing shorts, ones like we used to wear for basketball in the '50s, and a MSU football T-shirt. Nothing that would prepare him for an overnight stay.

The airline custodian successfully got Dick lined up with a hotel and a shuttle ride, explaining to the driver that Dick would need assistance. Nobody knows exactly what happened, but apparently Dick became disoriented and frantic in the middle of the ride, likely confused about his luggage and where he was going.

The driver later related that Dick got very aggressive and insisted on being returned to the airport. "He's a big man, and I wasn't going to cause trouble," said the driver. "He was scaring the other passengers, so I returned him to the airport."

There Dick stood, at 11:00 p.m., in a mostly empty airport with only a few dollars in his pocket, dressed in shorts and a T-shirt.

Carole and I were waiting at the Bemidji airport, anxious to begin what we hoped would be a successful visit with Dick at the cabin. Bemidji is a small airport with one gate, so it didn't take long to realize that Dick was not on the connecting flight—no bags, no Dick!

We approached the gate agent. "My brother was supposed to be on that flight. Can you help us figure out what happened?"

"If he's not here, he's probably still at Minneapolis–Saint Paul. A lot of the flights were late with the weather."

"I need to find him," I said with clear certainty. "He's likely confused."

"You'll have to call security at Minneapolis–Saint Paul," he replied, showing more interest in his paperwork than our dilemma.

Fueled by years of my own travel, my reaction to this typical, low-level customer concern by airlines boiled over instantly. "I don't know what you think your job is, but I'm not leaving this terminal until you help me find him. An airline custodian was supposed to be in charge." My voice level demonstrated complete dissatisfaction as I explained the situation.

It was then I saw the pilot and copilot attempting to bypass the disturbance to leave the terminal. "Captain— we need your help," I said, commanding his attention. Both men turned toward me. "We've got a problem with a missing passenger on your flight. As far as I'm concerned, everyone is going to stay here until we find out where he is."

I explained the situation, again, and finally saw a level of empathy and cooperation emerge from the captain's expression. My adrenaline started to cool, which coincided with a more relaxed approach with the airline crew.

After many phone calls by the captain—and how *I* was supposed to accomplish that on my own, as the gate agent originally suggested, I'll never know—we were connected to the security center at the Minneapolis–Saint Paul airport. The captain explained the situation. The security officer immediately began systematically scanning the airport through their surveillance system monitors for someone meeting Dick's description. At that point, we knew nothing of the hotel shuttle incident.

After thirty minutes of searching throughout this very large airport, the security officer said, "I think we have him. Is he wearing shorts and a green T-shirt?"

"Yeah, that's him." Mike had earlier relayed his frustration of not getting Dick to realize the weather in Minnesota would not be the same as in Indiana.

"It looks like he found a big piece of cardboard to lie on and is sound asleep in a stairwell."

With 20/20 hindsight about CTE, we now understand there's a decline in executive functioning, particularly in handling novel situations outside the norm. Even within the norm, optimal performance can't be expected with planning, decision-making, error correction, troubleshooting, and resisting temptation.

But at the time, my heart just sank. We had let him down. I felt as if we had lost our child in a shopping mall.

"What can we do?" My slumped shoulders and sad expression told the captain all he needed to know.

"Is there anyone you can contact?" he asked compassionately.

"There are two cousins in the area. I've tried both . . . left messages, but no reply."

"He's not going to hurt anything where he is," the security officer offered. "Why don't we just let him sleep? I'll have one of the officers give him a blanket and some bottled water. He'll keep a special eye on your brother and make sure he gets to his flight in the morning."

We realized it was all we could do, as the airport was a four-hour drive from Bemidji. "Okay, if you're sure," I said.

"He'll be fine. I'll make sure his luggage is on the flight with him."

"Thanks for your help," was all I could say.

* * *

I had a commitment for a Rotary presentation the next day, so Carole was on her own to meet the morning flight. It was on time. She saw Dick, but he didn't see her. His hair was a mess, his face was unshaven, and his shirt was dirty—homeless in appearance.

"Dick . . . Dick. I'm over here," she called.

He finally recognized her and made a beeline in her direction to give her a hug.

"Whoa, we need to get you to a shower—soon," she said, reacting instinctively with extended arms fending him off. Other passengers nearby overheard her comment and nodded in agreement. It wasn't just the body odor; it was the intense smell of urine.

Dick seemed oblivious to his circumstances and uncharacteristically articulate. "Boy, did I have fun last night. The flight people screwed everything up, and I had to figure everything out for them—where I could sleep, how I could make the flight today, everything. I don't think I would be here if I didn't tell everyone what they needed to do."

"Well, you're here now. That's what counts," Carole said. "Let's get your bags."

The drive from Bemidji to the cabin takes about forty minutes and goes through Cass Lake, making Teal's Market an easy stop.

"I need to go pick up a few supplies," she said as she pulled in to the grocery store. "Is there anything special you'd like, Dick?"

"Ice cream and cereal."

"Okay. You can stay in the car while I run in."

"I need to go too. You won't know what I need."

It occurred to Carole that Dick's need to come along was rooted in his inability to express what kind of ice cream and cereal he wanted. She reluctantly agreed.

In the store, Carole went to grab a cereal she normally purchased, but Dick stopped her with his hand.

"No, not that one. That one and that one," he said, pointing to Frosted Mini-Wheats and Raisin Bran. We learned later from Mike that he had become addicted to mixing the two every morning for years, but he failed in his attempt to name them.

Carole's private appraisal of Dick's current state, compared to his state just a few months earlier, was shocking. It's hard to describe a 240-pound, powerfully built man as childlike, but that's what he was. It was like shopping with a three-year-old.

"What kind of ice cream do you want?" she asked.

"Chocolate."

Carole removed a gallon from the freezer. Looking confused, Dick said, "Not that one. This one." He pointed enthusiastically at a gallon of mint chocolate chip.

* * *

Dick had showered and cleaned up by the time I arrived. I decided to let him just explore things on his own, but I kept a close eye once learning of Carole's assessment. He walked along the shoreline toward the property he had once owned, then developed and sold. He stopped and looked back at our place, then pointed to his old land that now had two beautiful homes on it.

"That was mine." Looking back at me, he said, "I like what you did better. Mom and Dad would be proud." Dick's dream of a lake home for his family had obviously derailed.

We walked more without talking. I noticed his gait was quite unstable—he was a stark contrast to the unbelievably coordinated athlete of his past.

"Do you want a ginger ale?" I asked, knowing it was his favorite, as we arrived back at our shoreline fire pit.

"Yes."

"You stay here. I'll bring it to you." He nodded, and I left.

I heard the panic in his moaning as I came out the back cabin door. I could hear a combination of frustration and strain—then I saw him on the ground. The wild look in his eyes was startling. It was the first time I saw him in complete panic.

"Fell," he said, pointing to the hand-hewn log benches. "Get up . . . get up!" he shouted.

I realized his lack of mobility, balance, and flexibility prevented him from getting up on his own. We interlocked our hands and arms, and it took all my weight and effort to get him vertical.

"There—you'll be all right," I said.

"Made these," he said, quickly shifting focus and pointing to the log benches, completely ignoring the falling episode. He slowly steadied himself.

At that moment, I knew everything we did that week would include the two of us together. I would try to resurrect every memory of his I could.

* * *

The next morning, we were off on a road trip—a perfect, sunny Minnesota day in the mid-seventies. We stopped at the Park Rapids Area Library first, where I did a presentation and signing for *In the Absence of Honor* on the way to our grandparents' cabin. I knew he would enjoy seeing me do my shtick, as he was proud of my writing accomplishments.

About twenty people were in the lower-level room set up for the event. I introduced Dick before the presentation started, then helped him sit in the back—his choice. Near the end of my presentation, someone asked about my participation on the 1965 MSU national championship football team, which was referenced in my bio. I gave a brief response, indicating my pride but not wanting to get off track.

Suddenly, Dick said in a loud, declarative tone, "I was the quarterback!"

It was awkward watching the audience turn toward him, not knowing how to react.

It didn't make any difference that he wasn't the quarterback of the '65 team. What was important was that his center-stage instinct was still alive. I talked with the audience a little about our time together on the field and just how good he was as "the quarterback." Within minutes, he drifted off into a nap.

* * *

The highlight of our growing up was the trips from Ohio to Stuart Lake, which wasn't far from Park Rapids and near the small town of Clitherall, population 112. "The Lake," as we called it back then, was the site of my grandparents' cabin. Classic north woods motif with wooden shutters on the porch; a hand pump water well; outdoor biffy; cast-iron, wood-fueled stove; and kerosene lanterns—a perfect Lands' End scenario.

After the book presentation, we found the old cabin location by taking a roundabout tour via East Battle Lake. The two-rut, single-lane road curved gently through an old cabin community that had not changed in sixty years.

"Look, Dick—remember that store?" I was trying to direct his attention, seeing as he seemed a little disoriented.

He was silent as he drank in the memories of where we used to get ice cream, candy bars, and fishing supplies as kids.

"Cabin . . . cabin," he said, pointing enthusiastically up the hill.

He was right; his long-term memory still functioned. The entrance lane to the cabin was at the top of the next hill, no more than two hundred yards away. It took just a few minutes to get the car parked and Dick out.

Sixty years had just been erased. It was just as if we had arrived in our 1953 Hudson and we were ten and twelve. I felt the excitement coursing through Dick, as it was the same feeling for me—almost a dreamlike quality of time travel back to our childhood. Dick stood there and just looked.

I tried to help him, as the grassy hill to the cabin was steep. He pushed my hand away. "Just here, too steep," he said, waving a finger at the hill's slope.

I didn't want to push it, as I knew the old cabin was gone and replaced with a new structure. Dick stood there, motionless, for over five minutes. Tears came to my eyes as I reflected on what must be his thoughts—a happy, acne-faced teen driving the wooden boat, catching the biggest fish, swimming, or just knowing that whatever he did would turn out perfect. Our parents reveled in our success, no matter the insignificance. Sometimes we just wandered the shore, catching turtles, seining minnows, or collecting cool rocks. I knew, for Dick, that these few minutes were priceless.

We returned to the car and slowly pulled away. But as we left, we were both distracted by the scene of the '40s-style, white-washed, stand-alone garage next door that literally hadn't changed. I stopped the car.

"Dick, look at that."

He nodded and smiled with a sense of comfort. A middle-aged man was doing repairs. We stopped and exchanged greetings, and he came to the car. Our conversation revealed that he was the grandson to the original owner, just as we were grandsons to the original owner next door.

As we were talking, Dick suddenly interjected, "I was the quarterback!"

The man—I forget his name—looked at Dick and politely offered a reply: "I'm sure you were very good." Nothing else was said as we waved and parted company.

Time on the road in the car had a cradle effect on Dick as we headed for Staples—our grandparents' primary home. As kids, we would fall into a pattern of counting telephone poles out of boredom. Today was different, as Dick slept most of the way.

I don't know why Dick wanted to first see the nursing home where Aunt Vera, our dad's sister, had resided and died. But he did, so that's where I headed. Once we entered the lobby, Dick became socially animated—not making much sense but friendly. Maybe Dick thought that if it was okay for Aunt Vera, it would be okay for him.

The situation seemed safe enough, so I left Dick and went back outside for a short break by myself on a bench in the sun. Before I knew it, fifteen minutes had passed. A man dressed in a suit and tie came out the door with a searching look on his face. We made eye contact and approached each other.

"We have an elderly gentleman wandering around inside that we can't seem to identify. Do you have any idea—"

"I'm sorry," I said, cutting him off. "That must be my brother."

I introduced myself, and after I explained the circumstances, the man laughed. "We knew he hadn't driven himself here," he said. "He seems perfectly at home, but he's not one of ours. Are you looking for a residence for him?"

"Soon, but not here. He lives with his son in Indiana. We stopped because our aunt Vera lived here for some time. I hope he didn't cause a problem."

"No, not in the least."

After collecting Dick, we stopped at our grandparents' home in downtown Staples, across from the town park and stream. We were lucky enough to see the owner on the porch preparing to leave. She allowed us to take a brief tour and was understanding as we meandered through her home. The smell and interior decor was the same—the paneled woodwork hadn't even been refurnished. Dick said nothing, but I could sense a visceral reaction as he attempted to capture the visions of youth, looking curiously at each room in the small bungalow house.

We parted Staples—mission accomplished. Dick fell into a deep sleep again as we headed back to Leech Lake. It had been a long day, but a successful one—at least I hoped it had been for Dick.

CHAPTER 20

Neuropsychological assessment scores
were in the "extremely low range," with a total score
less than 0.1 percent of the normative population.

The more Dick's world shrank, the more affirmation he needed. Yet in many instances, his memories of his business achievements were taking a back burner. Remaining center stage, however, were his football accomplishments.

Consequently, I set out on a campaign in 2010 to promote Dick's football legacy at Central Catholic. For decades, he had been on the short list of nominees for the Stark County High School Football Hall of Fame. I knew the 2011 induction ballot would be his last shot while still alive. I also knew how important the recognition would be for Dick, particularly considering there was so little else.

An outside observer could easily write this off as just one of many halls of fame honoring high school athletes across the country, but this one is different. Stark County is the home of professional football, with the Canton Bulldogs, led by the legendary Jim Thorpe. It's also the home of the Pro Football Hall of Fame, simply called "Canton" by many. The area has also been heralded as one of the greatest hotbeds of high school football ever across the country, with traditions including the Massillon Tigers and the Canton McKinley Bulldogs.

The mission of the Stark County High School Football Hall of Fame is to recognize excellence primarily at the high school level, although the list of enshrinees includes great athletes in the collegiate and professional ranks as well. My personal bias is for those from the Canton area who played at 1) Michigan State, including Wayne Fontes, George Saimes, Percy Snow, Tommy Hannon, and Chris Soehnlen; and 2) Central Catholic, including Alan Page, Bob Belden, Roger Duffy, Norm Nicola, and Coach John McVay (from both Central Catholic and Michigan State). Many greats of the game in the Pro Football Hall of Fame are also in the Stark County High School Football Hall of Fame. This list includes enshrinees Coach Paul Brown, Dan Dierdorf, Marion Motley, and Alan Page.

Dick's accomplishments in high school seemed to have gotten lost or weren't being given consideration. In reality, fifty years can obscure a lot, especially because stats and record keeping have changed so much. A single wing or T formation quarterback from the '50s and '60s can't compete with a quarterback whose stats are generated from the offenses and formations today. It's hard to compare achievements.

I decided to call Bob Belden—2009 enshrinee representing Central Catholic, Notre Dame, and the Dallas Cowboys—in order to get some advice. The Beldens have been family friends for many years, as well as leaders in the business community with the Belden Brick Company. We had breakfast at a local Bob Evans restaurant.

"There's no question of Dick being a deserving

nominee," he responded. "But it's not that easy."

He explained how the selection committee works. The committee has eight votes, and the public has two votes through a process of online voting. In order for a nominee to be inducted, he needs seven votes.

"Winning seven of eight votes from the selection committee is an honor reserved for only a select few . . . Alan Page, for example," Bob added.

"Interesting," I said. "It makes sense that the committee's prime objective is to ensure that only deserving nominees get selected. It prevents the honor from becoming a popularity contest."

"You got it." He smiled.

Over the next several months, my primary goal was to legitimately influence everyone I knew connected to the selection committee. My additional objective was to secure those two public votes. In the end, Dick received numerous written recommendations from existing enshrinees and selection committee members who knew his talent first-hand, having played with him or coached him. Players from high school and college—as well as friends and people from all over the United States who had never seen Dick play—responded to my barrage of e-mails asking for their help to influence the public vote with their ballot. Thank God for Al Gore and the Internet.

I was as serious as a heart attack in making this happen for Dick, and I personally prayed it would. Before the nomination period was over, a friend of mine said, "If I ever want to run for political office, I'll want you for my campaign manager."

Everyone's efforts and votes paid off. The final vote is never made public, but the committee head, Jim Porter of the *Canton Repository*, said, "There wasn't a question. We haven't seen that kind of overwhelming response in a long time."

Dick was in—the official induction ceremony would be held in the coming July.

* * *

One morning that September, leading up to the HOF, I was sitting, as usual, with a circle of friends after my workout at the Midtown Athletic Club in Palatine, Illinois. At the Breakfast Club, as we called ourselves, we drank some coffee and solved the problems of the world. Any topic was fair game—mostly general, but sometimes more personal.

I turned to Jay Lewkowitz, a Breakfast Club founding member. "Jay, is your shingle out this morning for some advice?" I asked.

Jay was a longtime friend and also the active owner of Oakton Place, an adult living community in Des Plaines where Carole's mother spent many years prior to her death. He was well known in Illinois for progressive approaches to adult living as well as for operating a first-rate center. I wanted to run our summer experiences with Dick by him.

"Always." Jay, like most people, loved being asked his opinion. He was also familiar with Dick's situation from previous discussions.

"My nephew Mike is concerned that Dick's living arrangement with him isn't working out and that we'll have to make other arrangements."

"What's the problem?"

I explained the long list of challenges, such as outside

influences, attempted escapes, aggressive confrontations, advancing care needs, poor decision-making, paranoia issues, and lack of socialization—to name a few.

"Mike works all day, and the task has become a little overwhelming. We've unsuccessfully tried part-time care options. Dick is big and powerful and hard to control. Coupled with his aggressiveness and outbursts, quite frankly, I think he scares people—including Mike."

"Are there facilities in the area with memory centers willing to take Dick?"

"His kids have done a nice job scoping the options. There's a place south of Warsaw called the Peabody that looks perfect," I said.

"So what's the problem?"

I laughed. "You know exactly what the problem is. We're not quite sure how to convince Dick that this is the right move. Plus, I think Mike is intimidated and unsure of the outcome if he gets aggressive."

"The care center can recommend professionals who can help in situations like this. But personally, I don't feel a straitjacket is the best way to introduce a new member to the adult care community." Jay paused to think. "He listens to you, doesn't he?"

"Other than Carole, I'm probably the only one. He's opened up more recently because of the hall of fame campaign. I've put a lot of effort into getting him enshrined this year."

Jay thought for another minute before the light bulb started to glow. "How about this?" he said. "Introduce the idea of the facility as more of a 'training center'—somewhere he can prepare himself for the induction . . . like a preseason camp."

It was pure genius. In truth, Dick was unsure how he would handle the award presentation. The array of physical, occupational, and speech therapy sessions he would receive at the Peabody could be positioned as "training."

"Dick has always loved training," I said.

We had a plan.

Mike organized the move a few weekends out so Carole and I could participate. It would be a lot of work that day. Carole spent time with Dick reviewing brochures while Mike and I got organized to make the move. The obvious challenge was to get Dick to want the move.

"Dick, think about it as training camp," I said. "They have everything you don't have here."

After pausing for a minute, he said, "Am I free to come and go?"

"Absolutely," I replied. "That's what independent living is." We knew we were pushing the envelope on the independent-living decision, but we were reassured because of the security and supervision level at the Peabody.

"Besides, things aren't really working out with Mike, are they?" I added.

He nodded in the affirmative. There was more silence, then he said, "You've got a lot to do if we're going to make everything happen today."

The rest of the day was a whirlwind effort, but it all came together. Dick's living arrangements at the Peabody would be very similar to his arrangement at Mike's, with the added inclusion of a kitchenette. Mike had purchased a new bed and covers that Dick was pleased with.

Members of the Peabody staff, as well as his new neighbors, tried their best to welcome Dick. But once he saw the residents' ages, he stiffened and said with disdain, "I'm not like them." Thankfully, he agreed to stay.

Dick worked hard with the staff as his "training" regimen took shape. The speech therapist was very cooperative to the idea of Dick writing out and practicing his hall of fame acceptance speech as a method to improve his communication skills, which were failing rapidly.

Within a short time, however, it was apparent that the independent part of his living arrangement was inappropriate. The assisted-living component needed to take over. Bathing, bowel and bladder management, functional mobility, food preparation, and personal hygiene all become issues requiring nursing care. We were surprised that he had become so unwilling and unable to perform many daily living activities so quickly after his arrival. We had thought the concept of independent living would be a motivator.

The first behavioral-psychological evaluation finally came in December 2010, due to adjustment issues. Challenges with speech, memory, anxiety, depression, and paranoia were noted, as was his shuffling gait. Still, CTE wasn't even a topic of discussion on their part at this point. Adult Protective Services had to get involved as well because Dick had said, "They only want my money," referring to Patty and Mike. Of course, the Peabody had to be responsive.

The same doctor conducted a follow-up evaluation three months later to determine competency. "Unfortunately, it was an easy determination," to quote the doctor's notes. The second evaluation showed a tremendous decline with "four out of five areas assessed showing results within the demented range, with relative weakness in memory . . ." In this last report, Dick claimed to have a "sister" he was "in business with, but scrambled it," and he said Patty lived "way out in the outskirts" when referring to her home in

Pennsylvania. The recommendation of "involving the POA in making significant decisions related to health, legal, or financial [matters]" didn't come as a shock to us.

I later found out Dick was still easily convincing a few high school friends that he was being taken advantage of. Maybe emotions do play tricks on the casual observer's ability to form clear judgments, but I still was offended by one of these "friends" who challenged me about what we were doing with Dick. Apparently, this one friend's two-hour visit made him an expert on what we had experienced over several years. Patty and Mike had to endure these comments as well. Dick's paranoia was growing, and he was not shy about expressing himself. Regardless of the rationale, this was hard on Patty, Mike, and me.

"Uncle Jim," Patty once said, "if they only knew the real situation of Dad's financial destitution, their judgment would be different. Dad's money disappeared long before we arrived."

Dick's Repeatable Battery for the Assessment of Neuropsychological Status scores were in the "extremely low range," with the total score less than 0.1 percent of the normative population. The report stated, "Qualitatively, perseveration in reference to 'being the quarterback' and difficulty with response inhibition were noted as frontal lobe related functions." In summary, "Results of this evaluation are consistent with a diagnosis of dementia, with possible multiple etiologies given the history of head injuries. There is evidence of impairment in memory, language, and executive functioning. The condition may be accompanied by depression."

Within this short period of evaluations, Dick ate by himself and otherwise refused to socialize, creating a shut-in effect—again. He fell and broke his hip, never leaving the rehab unit until the determination was made in March that physical and occupational therapy were no longer having an impact.

People at the Peabody tried their best to connect with Dick, with little success. Wanda was the only one who wouldn't admit defeat. She was a small lady, twenty years Dick's senior, and a self-appointed patient ombudsman. I wish I could remember her last name, as she deserved much credit in refusing to give up on Dick throughout his stay and made many bedside visits during his last days. She was Dick's angel, like Clarence in *It's a Wonderful Life*.

It was still hard to reconcile my big brother in this demented state. Our family history led us in the Parkinson's and Alzheimer's direction with Dick, even though we had been assured that neither was an inherited condition. "Multiple etiologies," however, was a new reference to me. And although Dick's head injuries were referenced in his evaluation, there was of course no specific mention of CTE, which in 2010 was only beginning to cross the public radar due to NFL players' deaths. I needed to learn more.

After some research, I learned CTE is so insidious that concussions in a young player's "glory years" can cause damage much later in life. CTE begins shrinking the brain long before the dementia is fully observable. I was starting to wonder if CTE had not only shrunk Dick's brain but his will to live—this hall of fame opportunity was all that kept him going. Ultimately, Dick's brain lost over 20 percent of its mass, and this certainly contributed to the startling and progressive decline in memory, planning skills, motor skills, language, interpersonal and social adjustment, grooming, and decision-making. Combined with the increase in anger, dementia, depression, and paranoia—to name a few—Dick was in a bad place.

If it is CTE, I thought, *why not me too?* We played the same sports in grade school, high school, and college under the same conditions, same coaches, and with about the same level of success.

The national media focused only on CTE in NFL players, as if they were the only people afflicted by the disease, which we know is not true. Clinton Jones—NFL player, All-American teammate from 1965 at MSU, and friend—typified this public perception when he learned about Dick's condition in a phone discussion. Even as someone who stays abreast of CTE issues, he said offhandedly, "And Dick didn't even play pro ball."

Clint didn't say it negatively, but it just confirmed the popular belief that CTE was only a result of the highest level of the game. This was understandable, with Mike Webster of the Pittsburgh Steelers being the first CTE diagnosis in 2002 and John Grimsley of the Houston Oilers being another pioneer case in 2008. To my knowledge, John was the first player from Canton with a documented case of CTE.

But even with our newspaper knowledge of CTE, we still weren't sure what was happening to Dick. All we knew was that it was happening fast. The evaluation findings and the free fall decline in Dick's condition just months after entering the Peabody were shocking, yet there was no professional diagnosis of CTE.

"We need to get ahead of this," Mike kept advising us as a family. "We've been one step behind in everything we've tried to do for Dad."

We all knew Mike was right. In reality, however, that horse had left the barn.

CHAPTER 21

"What we heard today was
the heart of a champion."

The day had finally come—Friday, July 22, 2011—the Stark County High School Football Hall of Fame Induction in Canton.

Dick's preparation for the induction ceremony had made little progress. His handwritten acceptance speech was simpleminded, with many, many errors. It needed "staff work" prior to the presentation, which I was all too happy to do. But my hope for Dick to give his own acceptance speech had vanished, as he struggled badly in constructing even simple sentences.

An odd caravan traveled to the event from Indiana to Ohio, including Dick, Patty, Mike, and a male nurse from the Peabody. Also along was Denise, the occupational therapist who had built a "relationship" with Dick. They all made the trip in a van equipped with a wheelchair.

Dick wore a braided bracelet with Denise's name embroidered into the design. He had told me he wanted to marry Denise. It was a strange relationship, emotional and physical, that in some respects was good for Dick, but it ultimately had its dark side. She once asked us if she could take a video camera into his apartment while she and Dick were together. That came shortly after an episode of Dick complaining to one of the nurses that "someone" had given him a blow job without his permission.

"It's beyond me how a reasonably attractive woman in her forties would want to have sex with a demented man wearing diapers," Carole proclaimed.

Patty was also disgusted with the whole arrangement. "This is embarrassing for Dad. He doesn't even know what's happening." She likened Denise to Bobbie Jean and other similarly minded women in his past. "The sad part is, at one point in time, he wanted to marry each of them. And he actually did marry Paula for her fourth marriage. It's not at all in keeping with who he is!"

Denise had been relieved of her responsibilities at the Peabody once the relationship was uncovered, but she continued as Dick's frequent "guest." We had to honor his patient-rights privileges, but we kept a very close eye on the situation—and had several face-to-face discussions with Denise to make sure she knew we were concerned. Regard-less, Dick wanted Denise at the hall of fame event. And so she was, adorned in a white bridesmaid-style, full-length dress for the induction dinner and presentation.

As the caravan arrived at the Holiday Inn with not much time to spare, I knew a discussion of a very direct nature was warranted to ensure damage control. I arranged to talk privately to Denise in her room.

"I respect my brother more than anyone, and you're here because he wants you here," I said. "But if you encourage him in any way to do anything that would cause embarrassment to Dick or the family, you'll have to answer to me. Are we clear? This event isn't about you!"

She didn't say anything the rest of the day. I probably scared the shit out of her, and maybe that was good. I've learned to trust my intuition.

From the moment Dick arrived at Skyland Pines, the venue for the event, he was back in the limelight again. We all enjoyed how he took to the attention and didn't let his inability to communicate verbally get in the way. We wanted to dress him in a sport coat for the affair, but he absolutely refused. He insisted on a MSU Football Players Association T-shirt I had bought for him a few years back, a pair of slacks, a belt, socks, and shoes. It was his day, and we weren't going to debate the wardrobe.

Mike Fay, Dick's good high school friend, attended the event. He and I couldn't help but note that no one else from Dick's former team attended, even though some still lived in the area. It was a complete lack of support. I didn't let it affect me at that time. The function was a little pricy, I reasoned, considering the Great Recession's lasting impact on the area.

I couldn't let it go in the weeks that followed, however, as other root causes surfaced in my mind. My guess was that Dick's history of unreasonable displays of wealth, his negative business dealings, and his ultracompetitive lifestyle—coupled with his growing negative behavior influenced by the dementia—had pushed people away long before the event. Had his disability been more visible and understandable, I'm sure people would have treated him differently. As it was, the silent, confusing nature of CTE created a lasting stigma.

Because I would be introducing Dick, we sat together at the head table. Next to us was Joe Sparma's widow,

Connie. Joe, representing Massillon High and Ohio State, died unexpectedly in 1986 after a triple-bypass surgery. Connie was Joe's lovely and classy high school sweetheart. She was kind enough to remember the stir the papers made in 1959 about how Joe and Dick—the two best senior quarterbacks in the state—never had the opportunity to face off in a game, even though they lived only a few miles apart. Two weeks prior to this induction, multiple articles had rehashed the same topic.

Each enshrinee was given time to talk to the audience of a few hundred. I had Dick's presentation prepared. I built my comments around the original draft he had worked on at the Peabody. After thanking many people for their support, I proceeded with the presentation, reading his own words on his behalf:

> *As a young man, many people contributed to my success in football.*
>
> *First, my parents played a huge role in developing the talent God gave me. They would be proud of this award.*
>
> *I called my mother, my angel. On Boy Scout trips she would pack food in plastic bags that I would take on canoe trips. She helped many people with her sewing, cooking, and unconditional love. This same love gave me the confidence to excel.*
>
> *My father always said, "If we need to get something done, we will, one way or another." His focus on goals helped him as an engineer for Goodyear Aircraft. This talent for achieving results became important for how I played football and approached life.*

CHAPTER 21

Second, I'd like to thank the many players and coaches that encouraged me to develop my talent on the field. In the end it is the team, players and coaches together, that deserves the recognition for my success. The precious memories of playing football, basketball, and baseball are still in my thoughts. I cherish the friendships I made.

Lastly, I am thankful for the positive impact that football has had in my life, including my education at Michigan State University, my personal life with friends and family, and my business career as owner of Mid-States Equipment. Football and athletics definitely played a big role in developing my leadership skills, both on and off the field.

Thank you again for this honor and for the contributions the sport of football, and the people involved, have made to my life.

When I finished, there was applause for Dick, but Dick was not to be denied. He motioned for me to give him the microphone. His attempt to stand from his wheelchair, with audible groans, disrupted the emcee, Todd Porter, from beginning his introduction of the next enshrinee.

It's hard to describe what happened next. Dick wanted to talk, but he couldn't. He was agitated and tense. He gestured for me to help him with the microphone. I did. The nurse and I held him upright as he attempted to speak.

His valor and courage broke everyone's heart. He couldn't communicate a single word—nothing of what was in his mind. The groans and guttural attempts were hardly recognizable, yet he continued for a full two minutes. He was met with applause and a standing ovation. He pumped his fist . . . the crowd responded.

Many said afterward that there wasn't a dry eye in the house. I told George Saimes before leaving, "What we heard today was the heart of a champion." He agreed.

The following day included the Ohio High School All-Star football game and the public introduction of the new hall of fame enshrinees. Carole and I didn't stay, leaving for the long drive back to Chicago. We felt Dick's celebration would be best enjoyed as time alone with Patty and Mike. The Denise factor would somehow have to take care of itself.

Mike told me that Dick tired quite a bit at the game but still insisted on visiting our parents' joint gravesite before returning to the Holiday Inn for dinner. Part of the urgency in Dick's mind was the need to see the location of his own plot, as he wanted it to be near Mom and Dad's.

Disaster was about to strike—Mike and Patty couldn't locate Mom and Dad's gravestone at the large Sunset Hills cemetery. It was late on Saturday, and the attendant who normally assisted visitors had gone home. Mike moved quickly while he attempted to locate the gravesite, and Patty tried her best to keep her dad calm.

"We don't have all night!" Dick yelled in Mike's direction through garbled articulation. Now that the pressure of the induction presentation was gone, his speaking ability had temporarily returned somewhat.

"Hang on, Dad. I haven't been here in over ten years." A frantic tone crept into Mike's voice as he moved and scanned for some kind of landmark—a tree, a bend in the road, anything to trigger his memory.

"Goddammit, Mike. Can't you do anything?" Dick strained in his wheelchair, trying to get out. Fists were waving, and spittle came out of his mouth as he continued ranting.

"Dad, it's been ten years since any of us have been here. Be patient," Mike pleaded.

"Find 'em, I said! I'm not going to get another chance."

Patty made a timing mistake. "Dad, it's not a big deal. Your plot won't be right next to theirs, anyway."

"That's what I wanted!" he screamed. "You're no better than he is!" he shouted, pointing an accusing finger at Mike. "That's all I wanted, and you messed that up too."

"Dad," Patty replied. "That's not fair. There were no plots available next to Grandma's and Grandpa's. What were we supposed to do? Dig someone up?"

"Just get me out of here! I don't want anything to do with you two," Dick said, hurling one more destructive insult at his kids.

"We'll come back tomorrow before going home. I'll call Uncle Jim. Maybe he can help," Mike said with that all-too-familiar tone of defeat when trying to please his dad.

The sun was setting as Mike called me. Their party was loading back into the van. Carole and I were in the car on our way back to Chicago.

"Hi, Uncle Jim."

"Hey, Mike. What's up? A good day with your dad, I hope."

"Shit, I'm tired of this. Am I supposed to be perfect?" he said in frustration.

"What happened?"

Mike related the meltdown from not finding the gravesites. "The whole weekend will be a waste if I can't find them," he said. "We're heading back to the hotel now, but maybe you can help me know where to go when we try again tomorrow."

"Don't feel bad, Mike. I had the same problem just a year ago. Are you at the cemetery right now?" I asked.

"No. We're on our way back to the hotel."

"How do you want me to help?"

"I was thinking I could come to the cemetery early on my own tomorrow, and maybe I can find the gravestones with you on the phone."

"Sounds like a plan. Other than that, how's the rest of the party going?" I asked.

"Without your help, this never would have happened. Dad needed this hall of fame validation badly. I'm not sure how long he'll remember it, though. He's failing fast in every area. I can tell you he's absolutely exhausted right now. He's already asleep in the car."

"Hang in there. You're a good son. One more day to go."

Early the next morning, after getting our bearings, Mike and I located the site. He returned to the hotel, had breakfast, and checked out.

After the van was packed and everyone aboard, they headed back toward the cemetery. You could cut the anticipation with a knife. It was a nice summer day in Canton, and the rolling terrain of Sunset Hills was calming. Mike was brimming with confidence; Dick was sullen, expecting the worst. Everyone was thinking, *Does Mike have it right?*

The nurse wheeled Dick, following Mike's directions, directly to Mom and Dad's gravesite.

Dick nodded approvingly. "Where's mine?"

"Over here, Dad, by the tree. It has a nice view of Grandma and Grandpa," Mike answered.

Once Dick overlooked his own plot, with its acceptable relationship to our parents' plot, he went still. Everyone knew not to interrupt. He seemed to be praying, thanking his parents for all they had done. And then more silence. It wasn't long before he started crying. The outburst of emotion escalated to uncontrollable sobs, with animated arm movements of resignation.

I wish Carole and I hadn't returned early to Chicago, as it was foreseeable that Dick would experience a big letdown once the hall of fame weekend was over. I probably could have helped interpret for the others, who were somewhat bewildered by his reaction at the cemetery.

There's no question in my mind that he felt his life had not gone as planned and that he had, in some respects, let his parents down. He had run out of time. His need for perfection was a harsh and unfair bar of achievement, but that was Dick.

At that moment, I'm sure he felt the weight of some despair. Yet I also know he must have recognized the incredible gift of two parents who loved him unconditionally. He knew he would join them soon.

CHAPTER 22

Mike and Patty were delivered
the ultimate insult later in 2011.

I made a surprise visit to the Peabody in the fall of 2011. When I arrived, Dick was on a phone call, so I sat down and waited for him to finish. I could tell it was a female voice, either Bridget or Paula was my guess. Whoever it was, she was making more plans to try moving him back to Ohio.

He looked at me with very stern eyes and in mid-discussion yelled, "Get the hell out of here. Get the hell out of here!"

I removed myself until the call was over, then returned. "Are you all right?" I asked. Dick had never been this abusive to me.

"Go away. Just go away."

"Do you know who I am?"

He didn't answer. He just bowed his head, indicating he wasn't quite sure.

"Are you confused about who I am?" I asked again.

He nodded. His eyes expressed a new level of despair, a hopelessness that was heartbreaking. It seemed, for just a moment, that he knew what life once was and that it was now gone. I thought, *Would I be any different?*

Dick had mistaken me for Mike. Now I knew firsthand what frustration it was to walk in Mike's and Patty's shoes.

At that time, we didn't know about anosognosia. Later, through our relationship with the Boston University Center for the Study of Traumatic Encephalopathy, where Dick's brain was donated for research in 2012, we learned that anosognosia sometimes manifests in Alzheimer's and CTE dementia patients. It's a condition where the patient does not know he or she has a serious psychiatric illness. This presents a tremendous challenge to family members and caregivers.

Anosognosia is not the equivalent of psychological denial. It is a malfunction in the brain's frontal lobe, diminishing the person's ability to organize information and interpret experiences. For Dick, compounding this frontal lobe malfunction was a likely amygdala malfunction that limited his control of emotional reactions. This explains why our efforts to help Dick were frequently met with denial, frustration, and anger. Unfortunately, we knew about this condition too late.

Under the veil of anosognosia for years, Dick must have felt it was the people and circumstances around him that were wrong—not him. Why should he have to deal with the Peabody, the related medical therapy appointments, the IRS, and all the other family BS?

Patty and Mike were ultimately robbed of everything connecting them to their dad—but their dad couldn't possibly comprehend that fact. They couldn't convey the truth to him, as the truth had become unreachable, deluded, and bastardized.

And as cruel as these consequences were, nothing compared to the blind, cold, and deliberate finality that escaped all reason and hope of any improvement or recovery for him.

It was about 9:00 p.m., and I knew he was tired. So with whatever time we had left, I just rubbed his shoulders and talked about Michigan State football. God, I couldn't believe how firm and developed his shoulder muscles still were. As we talked, the tension left, and he fell asleep.

* * *

Sometime in 2011, I read a CNN news report that stopped me cold. Dave Duerson had been a fixture as a safety on the Chicago Bears defense. He committed suicide by shooting himself in the chest, avoiding any destruction to his brain. His suicide note read, "My mind slips. Thoughts get crossed. Cannot find my words . . . I think something is seriously damaged in my brain."

> Today, scientists announced that Duerson's brain tissue showed "moderately advanced" evidence of chronic traumatic encephalopathy, a dementia-like brain disease afflicting athletes exposed to repeated brain trauma.
>
> "Dave Duerson had classic pathology of CTE and no evidence of any other disease," said Dr. Ann McKee, a neuropathologist with the Bedford VA Medical Center and co-director of the Boston University School of Medicine Center for the Study

of Traumatic Encephalopathy. "He had severe involvement of areas that control judgment, inhibition, impulse control, mood and memory."

"Wow," I said out loud. "That's it!" This article finally connected all the dots for me.

I called Mike and Patty with my discovery. Mike made immediate contact with the Boston University School of Medicine to see if they were looking for brain donations from non-NFL players. Dr. Ann McKee's research clearly indicated that the problem of concussions may be much broader than professional sports.

They were very open to our call and thrilled to include Dick's brain, when the time came. We learned CTE could be definitively diagnosed only through a postmortem examination. Chris Nowinski—head of the Sports Legacy Institute, the nonprofit partner with the center—was charged with making contact with potential donor families, so he helped us through the process.

* * *

As if circumstances hadn't become confused enough, Mike and Patty were delivered the ultimate insult in October 2011: a court action initiated by Bridget Svendsen, Paula's granddaughter, for her appointment as Dick's guardian.

"This is a new low," I told Carole. "Are these people just stupid?"

Apparently, Bridget's idea was to have Dick live with her and her boyfriend—the father of her two children but yet to commit as a husband. The petition followed a failed attempt to remove Dick from the Peabody several months earlier when Bridget and her boyfriend simply showed up and tried to walk Dick out the door.

I never saw the originating document she filed with the court. Taking the high road, I can only surmise an extreme level of naïveté in feeling she could do a better job than the combined efforts of Mike, Patty, the professional staff at the Peabody, Carole, and me. Taking the low road, one could easily conjecture that she wanted to move Dick in with her so she could gain control of his Social Security income and remaining assets. My guess is that Paula was the puppet master behind the scene, wanting the Ellicottville home back in her grasp for a place to put her snowmen art collection back on display.

Had their concern for Dick been genuine, they presumably would have, at a minimum, initiated contact with Carole and me. It never happened—pretty damning evidence in my opinion.

The petition was extremely selfish, either way. Dick had had numerous phone discussions with Bridget and Paula that focused on removing him from the Peabody any way they could. Any reasonably bright person had to realize these antics created an unwarranted agitation for Dick, further reducing his quality of life. Several psychiatric examinations had already determined him incompetent. He was not capable of dealing with this level of conflict. His emotions were in complete chaos.

The Wabash County Circuit Court sent a notice of a hearing set for January 4, 2012. In response, our brother, John, sent a letter objecting to Bridget's petition and supporting Mike and Patty as Dick's guardians. I, of course, sent a letter as well. In truth, I was so angry that I would have preferred to appear in person to present my position on the matter.

> *Richard J. Proebstle (CAUSE NO: 85C01-1110-GU-57) is my older brother by two years. It comes as a shock to me that Bridget Svendsen has entered a petition for Appointment of Guardianship of an Incapacitated Adult. I have personally been consistently involved with Dick's situation over the last several years, including the time prior to the divorce from his ex-wife, Paula, who is the grandmother of Bridget. I would be happy to appear in court to testify personally what I witnessed firsthand in the decline of their relationship and the lack of care received during the onset of his dementia.*
>
> *More importantly, I am an extremely strong advocate of the responsible approach that both Patty Pae and Michael Proebstle (Dick's children) have taken in support of their father; both emotionally, physically, and financially. There is no aspect of this care that I am not intimately familiar with firsthand. There is no aspect of their care that my wife, Carole Proebstle, Psy.D, and I haven't given full approval to, particularly considering the many challenges involved. Mike and Patty have been open and solicitous of our advice throughout these recent years. As an older brother, Dick and I are very close, and there isn't anything I wouldn't do to ensure his well-being. Any parent would be proud of the support received from Mike and Patty.*

*I would like to be clear in my statement that
I am not in favor of any non-family member
becoming responsible for the affairs of my brother,
particularly considering the admirable job that Mike
and Patty are already doing. The best for Dick is to
continue to support Mike and Patty in the yeoman's
effort they've already accomplished in managing
their dad's care.*

The court's decision was swift: any move for guardianship in Bridget's favor was vacated.

It's impossible to say how much stress the battle over guardianship placed on Dick, but it's reasonable to think it lowered his quality of life. It also placed an unnecessary load of stress on Patty and Mike, creating a level of discord that could not have been healthy for Dick.

His circumstances never improved.

CHAPTER 23

"Hospice just left, and they said
Dad may go at any time."

It seems like just yesterday that Carole and I were visiting with Dick after his terrifying escapade of the emergency visit to the hospital, when he thought the "bad men" had taken him. I feel as if I could reach out and touch that day. The frightened look on his face with the beads of sweat shimmering on his brow was shocking, as I had never seen Dick afraid of anything. Experiencing his own fear for the first time is likely the trigger for Dick's panic.

I want to hold on to that memory, because he's still alive in it—there's still time for us to do something to help.

* * *

"Uncle Jim," Mike said on the phone that Sunday evening.

"Yeah, Mike. What's up?" I replied while sitting in our family room, sipping my all-too-regular gin and tonic.

Mike's tone was in control but very resigned. "Hospice

just left, and they said Dad may go at any time. He's in a coma, and they don't expect him to come out of it."

"How can that be? This is way too fast." My thoughts of the strength in his muscles and the power in his emotions told me this just couldn't be true. "He's got too much fight left."

"That's what Patty and I thought too."

"How much time do they give him?" I asked.

"Maybe tomorrow, possibly the next day."

"We'll be there as soon as we can tomorrow. Are you and Patty all right?"

"We'll be fine. Our plan is to stay with Dad through the night. I have to take Patty to the airport tomorrow, and then I'll return. There's really nothing anyone can do for him other than pray." I could hear the engineer in Mike's logic as he moved himself step by step through the process of preparing for his dad's death.

"Hang in there. We'll call you from the road in the morning to give you an ETA."

* * *

The number of trips to Indiana over the last few years became a blur. This time as we drove, Carole and I prepared ourselves to believe that today would be the day.

"I knew this day would come, but he's only sixty-nine, for Christ's sake," I said rhetorically, my hands gripping the steering wheel with the tension of an aftershock.

When we reached the Peabody, Dick was lying in bed in a coma, partially covered with a sheet, propped up, head back, gasping with every breath.

"Goddammit," I said with resignation as I reached his bedside.

I put my hands on his chest and felt the fitful rhythm of shallow breaths. Yet even in this diminished condition, his physical structure was solid. I remembered the shell of my mother's body after suffering with years of Alzheimer's and Parkinson's—this was completely different.

I wanted to be strong for Dick, but my emotions controlled the day as I wept for the loss of the life I knew he wanted to live.

Mike lifted the sheets by his ankles and showed me the deep-purple skin tissue, a telltale sign of lack of circulation. "The hospice lady told me to watch for this."

I put my hands on his knees. "They are cool."

"We'll see the continued discoloration in the extremities as the process of shutting down continues," Mike said. "According to the hospice lady, the reptilian brain stem is starting to take final control over events. She said that the heart will protect itself by restricting its range of blood flow . . . The extremities are the first to be affected. Ultimately, the brain stem is the last to go."

Carole, Mike, and I spent the day with Dick, telling stories, sharing family photo albums, crying, massaging his tight muscles, playing music—anything we could do to create an environment of comfort, knowing he could go at any minute. He was never left alone as we alternated meal breaks and our personal time to just get up and move around.

Patty had already left for home by the time we arrived. I talked with her on the phone to make sure she was all right.

She was distraught, and it was obvious she had been crying for some time.

"I wanted to stay, Uncle Jim, but I just can't stand

losing him. I don't think I've ever really had him close as an adult, and now I never will. I don't want to see him go."

Dick was like a warrior holding his ground in the face of insurmountable odds—like the Spartan he was, keeping the Persian king Xerxes from victory at the battle of Thermopylae in ancient Greece. The war inside his body came to a standstill, and his condition held ground. Before we knew it, the nurses were changing for the night shift.

We had assumed Dick would pass sometime that day, so Carole and I hadn't brought any personal items or made hotel arrangements.

"What do you want to do?" Carole asked me.

"I'm not leaving. Let me see how the staff handles this. We can't be the first to find themselves in this situation."

A local motel had a vacancy, but I was not going to leave. The nurses were very cooperative in making us comfortable in chairs and couches with blankets for the night. I decided to stay with Dick and sleep in his La-Z-Boy next to his bed. Carole made herself a spot in the lounge area. Mike lived close by, so he went home with the promise we would call immediately when his dad's condition changed. But nothing happened all night.

Midway through our vigil, Carole awoke to check on Dick. She actually laughed when she came into the room. There Dick was, flat on his back, covers up around his neck, mouth open, and snoring. There I was, flat on my back, covers up around my neck, mouth open, and snoring. Carole told the nurse they should put a Post-it note on my forehead identifying me as the "visiting brother," just in case of confusion in a medical emergency.

The next day, Tuesday, came and went still without any change in Dick's condition. Throughout each shift change, the staff related stories about Dick and how proud they were to have such a famous athlete and hall of fame enshrinee in their care. Both the hospice personnel and the nursing staff's personal attention to "who Dick was" told of the professional care provided by the Peabody.

At first, it appeared to be a mechanical approach to hospice care, but I was mistaken. The process was thorough and efficient, for sure. But with each nurse came tenderness toward the human condition—not just Dick's but ours, as well. They experience death and suffering each day, enough to induce depression in any of us. But their charter isn't to fall into the downward cycle of sadness and despair but to raise the level of dignity for each person in their care. I recognized in this staff a belief I've long held: it is a parallel gift to celebrate a person's entry into life as it is to have the honor in helping a person transition out of life.

"He is part of our family," one nurse said with true conviction.

Wednesday came and went. After three days of being on watch, our presence was now preceded by a distinctly ripe odor. The absence of toothbrushes, fresh clothes, or showers was taking its toll.

After breakfast on Thursday morning, I told Carole, "I think Dick's enjoying the attention . . . but we may kill him with our smell."

With his condition holding steady, we decided to make a quick run back to Chicago at 1:00 p.m. We missed the rush traffic and had a quiet meal when we arrived home. By 7:00 p.m., I was ready to head back to the Peabody, equipped with the necessary personal items to see things through.

"Are you sure you don't want me to go with you?" Carole asked. She herself had reached closure and didn't need to return, but she offered to come for support.

"I'm fine. At this point, it's more of a personal journey, anyway."

"Are you sure?" she persisted.

"I'm good—don't worry."

"Give me a call when you get there. I do worry." The sleepless nights and long hours on the road had her more concerned about my driving than anything.

"I will." After giving her a kiss, I was gone.

* * *

It was around 10:00 p.m., Thursday, May 17, just a short distance on Route 30 nearing Warsaw. The traffic became very light. I had the radio on a soft-rock station as I reviewed the "game films" of my life with Dick.

Clearly, there were ups and downs, but what stuck with me most was the core of who he always was—loyal, generous, hardworking, smart. A competitor and team-mate. I experienced these parts of him more than anything as a brother.

I smiled, recalling Dick's reaction to the road contractor fiasco on his Minnesota property years ago. After many years of ignoring my letter and objections, he ultimately accepted the reality that he had mishandled events. His self-imposed penance was to spend many hours on his Bobcat, rebuilding one hundred yards of my entryway access road. Actions, not words, were his strength of character.

We live in an amazing world where each person leaves a dynamic mark—a small pebble dropped in a pond, creating thousands of concentric circles—by how we live our life. I felt Christ's presence with Dick as I drove, as He had been with us over the last three days.

And then, my cell phone rang. I pulled over to focus on the call—it was from the Peabody.

"Is this Mr. Proebstle?" the caller asked.

"Yes, it is."

I knew what was coming, and I didn't want to hear it. I wanted to be with him when he left.

"This is Dick's nurse at the Peabody. Your brother passed on ten minutes ago."

The grip inside me was an overwhelming sense of loss. I was only thirty minutes from the Peabody. *Why couldn't I have left earlier to return?*

"Did he suffer?" I asked.

"No . . . not at all. His passing was very easy. He never regained consciousness and basically held his own until his heart just stopped. This frequently happens, when the person dying waits to be alone in order to die, as if not to disappoint the loved ones who are with him. There's just nothing you could have done."

Nothing I could have done? I thought. I wanted to scream. What about the years he suffered in frustration, not knowing anything was wrong with him? What about his private struggle with business decisions he was no longer able to make? What about the change from "Dick" to "Richard" that marked a lowering of personal standards no one could account for? What about the migraines? What about the destructive relationship with Mike and Patty? *Certainly there was something I could have done!* I thought.

"I'm just a few miles away. Should I still come? I mean, is there anything I can do now?"

"No. We're preparing him for the coroner right now,

and they should be here in minutes. We already talked with Mike, and the medical procedure for the donation of his brain needs to happen quickly in order for it to arrive at Boston University Medical tomorrow."

"Thank you," I said. "You've all been very helpful with Dick. The family is grateful."

I disconnected the call and just sat in an empty used-furniture store parking lot, with its dim area light glowing off to my left. The biggest person from my sixty-seven years on this earth was gone. The floodgates opened, and it felt as if the tears of a lifetime were draining from my soul.

My heart was broken.

EPILOGUE

Capturing this story has been quite a journey—not one I fully expected. I was angry when I first started the project. Angry with how people treated Dick, when his dementia was obvious. Angry because of the years wasted not knowing what CTE was. Angry with myself for judging Dick and not looking deeper at his symptoms. Angry with people taking advantage of Dick's diminishing capacity. Angry for losing a brother. Angry that his kids took unfair criticism in handling their dad's situation. And angry we couldn't help more.

What I'm not angry about, however, is the sport of football itself. This may seem odd to many, as the concussions he received as a player were what caused his CTE.

I would venture to say that any one of us who played for a successful high school, college, or professional program has a deep respect for the sport of football and the lifelong lessons that shaped our lives.

We all played under the mantra of "The great ones play hurt." In reality, there are many "hurts" in life that each of us has to "play through." The physical pain from football is nothing more than the by-product of giving it our best—and hopefully winning. It helps us endure and prepare for the inevitable pains that come with life, whether physical, emotional, psychological, financial, or spiritual. To be sure, our faith in whatever we believe in will be tested in life.

In my opinion, football is the greatest sport alive. Unfortunately, we now know the unintended impact of the collisions delivered to the head—Chronic Traumatic

Encephalopathy (CTE). Helmets are designed to protect the skull, not the brain. How unfair is it that the "dings," "bell-ringings," and concussions received in our youth may lead to CTE dementia, which will jeopardize the quality of life—and jeopardize life itself—as we get older?

So what do we do? We evolve. The sport evolves. We continue to test ourselves through competition that brings the best out in all of us, but we do so knowing we have to make it safer for the players. We can't run from every possibility of getting hurt. That's not a successful strategy for life. But we can be smart in order to protect players from traumatic brain injuries. We can accomplish this through research, education, new rules for coaches and players, better equipment and technology, sideline diagnostic procedures, and changes in the game, to name a few. This will require the collective effort of the football community at all levels—equipment providers, technology partners, medical research, coaches, players, public policy, and parents. (See the "Where Do We Go from Here?" appendix.)

Everything evolves, and so will football. But we need to ensure that the critical elements of player safety are at the forefront of that change.

While the journey of writing this book began with my own confusion, sadness, and anger, I have also experienced much happiness and gratitude along the way. What I am most thankful for in this journey are the few friends who stood by Dick and didn't judge: Jane (Matthews) Steiner, Jim Bray, Mike Fay, Terry Glarner, George Saimes, and John Walsh. I am happy Dick experienced the recognition of his talents in football through his enshrinement in the Stark County High School Football Hall of Fame before his death. I am happy for Patty and Mike, as their journey with

CTE has come to an end. They are content in the acceptance that the symptoms of the disease—such as anger, outbursts, paranoia, distrust, bad decisions, and disapproval—are only just that: symptoms of a disease and not a reflection of the dad they once knew and who loved them.

Lastly, this journey has been in hope that this story of amateur football will help reinforce our understanding of the potential impact of concussions and CTE, in order to build awareness with our friends and loved ones who are playing football or have played football. It is my desire that *Unintended Impact: One Athlete's Journey from Concussions in Amateur Football to CTE Dementia* will join a growing body of work to help preserve the phenomenal sport of football by making it safer for the players.

Many people and organizations are seeking a better understanding of concussions through research. In the minds and experience of our family, none compare to Boston University Medical Center for the Study of Traumatic Encephalopathy, with the research staff of Dr. Ann McKee and Dr. Robert A. Stern, led by Dr. Robert C. Cantu. Working closely with the center is the Sports Legacy Institute, led by Chris Nowinski, author of *Head Games* and advocate in the fight for player safety in contact sports. The Sports Legacy Institute staff provided us professional, caring, and educational support throughout the process of harvesting Dick's brain. (For more information, visit www.bu.edu/cte and www.sportslegacy.org.)

WHERE DO WE GO FROM HERE?
A Discussion for Parents, Coaches, Fans, and More

As parents, we naturally want our children to grow up to be responsible adults. That unfortunately involves their learning how to handle successes, disappointments, and failures. Sports are custom designed for this task.

We're now learning, however, that concussions can come from soccer to baseball to football, with varying risk components attached. Is there no place that's safe? In my own experience, the least likely place for "safety" would have been for me doing nothing. Not being involved in football, with the terrific coaches I had, would have robbed me of the lessons I learned in my development as a young man.

As parents, we can take certain steps to support and encourage our children in football:

1. Make sure our children are playing sports because they want to play, not because we're reliving our lives through them.

2. Help them be physically prepared to play. Many ten-year-olds are not ready for tackle football, for example.

3. Check out the coaches' credentials and be involved enough to know if these are the kind of people and programs we want influencing our children.

4. Make playing football a privilege, subject to
   the accomplishment of their best efforts in the
   classroom.

* * *

As a coach or part of a coaching staff, you naturally want to
win, develop a positive reputation for your program, develop
your athletes into positive young men and women, and build
success for yourself in your chosen career. Everything in
sports is evolving, though, and that must include your philos-
ophy, training methods, practice drills, player education,
equipment, return-to-play policies, and attitude. If the old
culture survives in football, especially, the sport will die.

Many universities and athletic programs throughout
the United States are struggling with the need to change
methods in regards to CTE and player safety. If you need a
positive-proof example of success, just reference what's in
place at Michigan State University's football program. The
MSU Concussion Consortium has partnered with Coach
Mark Dantonio and his football staff to develop an impres-
sive model to protect players from the negative impacts of
concussions:

1. The Concussion Consortium includes top-level
   university involvement from Lou Anna Simon,
   president, and Mark Hollis, athletic director.

2. All coaches are actively involved in concussion
   education.

3. Under the direction of David Kaufman, DO, advanced research is being conducted in concussions by Sally Nogle, PhD; Tracy Covassin, PhD; and David Zhu, PhD. All incoming freshman football athletes are given the opportunity to participate in a baseline MRI study to be used for treatment of potential concussions as well as for ongoing research to determine objective radioactive biomarkers.

4. David Kaufman, DO—chair of the MSU Department of Neurology and Ophthalmology and department head at Sparrow Neurosciences Center—is on the sidelines during every football game.

5. Under the direction of Sally Nogle, PhD, athletic trainers support all practice and game scenarios for all sports and are certified in providing sideline judgment in dealing with concussions.

6. Return-to-play guidelines for players receiving concussions are well developed and adhered to by the coaching staff. ImPACT (Immediate Post-Concussion Assessment and Cognitive Testing) is used to objectively measure cognitive function in concussed athletes and to track healing and recovery.

7. Practice strategies for reducing the exposure to collisions and concussions are continually reviewed to improve player safety.

8. There is a change away from the culture of "the great ones play hurt" to a culture of players openly showing concern for injured teammates— recognizing that allowing an injured player to stay in the game hurts the team and the player.

For coaches concerned about how concussion safety procedures affect the team's performance and success, consider the successful track record of the MSU Spartan football program since Dantonio became head coach in 2007. A Big Ten Championship (2013), Rose Bowl performance (2014), 11–2 season (2014), and Cotton Bowl victory (2015) would certainly indicate that paying attention to player safety will not dumb down the level of play on Saturday.

* * *

Equipment manufacturers must lead the charge in developing new technologies, materials, and applications for safer helmets. With hindsight, it's easy to recognize how a person's life can be destroyed through a simple event such as a concussion. Given this reality and the popularity of football, it's a certainty that there's a financial return for the innovator able to design headgear to protect the brain, as well as the skull, in a collision. It's likely that every helmet produced—from biking, to skiing and snowboarding, to baseball, to hockey, to football—will be subject to replacement once a solution is discovered.

* * *

Legislators know that player safety has taken a preeminent position moving forward. It's easy to follow the evolution of the $765 million lawsuit at the professional level of football. But can we see the potential consequence of a similar action against the NCAA? Buried in the unionization efforts of the Northwestern football team is an issue of player safety. The extension of this legislative logic is for each state to have an effective concussion law on the books that supports player safety at the grade school and high school level. This concept became clear to me when I heard Chris Nowinski say, "At these early ages, 'informed consent' isn't always a realistic concept."

* * *

And as fans, we all love the action—that's why we get excited about football. We relate to the feel of competition, we're in awe as we witness excellence, or, possibly, we have the fleeting connection that that could have been us.

Regardless of what motivates us as fans, let's remember that while many young people are gifted with skills, only a very few have the talent to go pro. This means most young athletes will work next to us in our careers and share the same excitement for the game, the same commitment to excellence—better for their experience. They will be men and women active in their jobs, building relationships, and raising their own families. All of this can happen success-fully, but only if their brains are still functioning effectively!

DICK'S EULOGY

Born: June 8, 1942 • Died: May 17, 2012

I am honored greatly to be able to express myself with you on behalf of my brother Dick. But first, I would like to thank each of you for your presence here and the wonderful compassion and kindnesses in your cards, e-mails, and phone calls to the family. They really did make a difference.

In 2005, Steven Jobs addressed the Stanford University graduation class, and in his commencement address he was quoted as saying, "No one wants to die. Even people who want to go to heaven don't want to die to get there." He expanded the point by saying, "Death is very likely the single best invention of Life. It is Life's change agent." In his conclusion, he said, "Remembering that you are going to die is the best way I know to avoid the trap of thinking you have something to lose. You are already naked. There is no reason not to follow your heart."

I started thinking about this more. While the physical and metaphysical changes for Dick are self-apparent, changes that came as a by-product of his death became interesting. I'd like to mention a few:

1. Mike and Patty and Carole and I were privileged to tag-team what turned out to be a weeklong vigil with Dick. During that time, it became very apparent as to how much Mike and Patty had grown into their responsibilities in managing the

complication of Dick's affairs over the last few years—right through until today, when we say farewell. They loved their father very much, as he loved them.

2. I changed because Dick's situation gave me an opportunity over the last few years to give back to a brother who gave so much to me. Our connection at all stages in life was very strong. It was Carole, however, who noticed that despite my changes, Dick and I had grown to look more and more alike. She came into Dick's room at the Peabody the night before he died. I was asleep on a recliner chair next to Dick's bed. My head was back, mouth open, breathing heavily—just as Dick's was. Carole laughed out loud with how much we looked alike and nearly put a Post-it note on my forehead saying, "This is the visiting brother . . . do not medicate."

3. Dick was a challenging resident in the beginning at the Peabody. I saw their staff change over time, however, and continually make the second effort in order to make Dick feel at home. It was heartwarming to hear their stories while we were there as to how Dick had become part of their family.

4. Some of you know that Dick's brain has been donated to Boston University, where leading research is being conducted into Chronic Traumatic Encephalopathy, or CTE, dementia. It's a growing concern for players receiving repetitive

head concussions in contact sports and can only
be diagnosed postmortem. Isn't this just classic
Dick Proebstle overachievement? His greatest
contribution in sports may be yet to come . . . after
his death. Hopefully, it will facilitate change.

5. Throughout the process of Dick's death, family and
friends, like yourselves, made comments that aren't
a normal part of day-to-day living. Sometimes
these acts of love and compassion go unsaid in
our lives, but not this time. I was particularly
comforted by everyone in my immediate family
and, in particular, by a voice mail message from my
son, Jeff, which I will probably never erase.

6. Lastly, when considering these changes—and I'm
sure there are many others—the ultimate question
arises . . . Are we really going to change? Will we
actually become better as a result of reflecting on
the experiences of the death of someone we love?

As a brother, I look at Dick's role in life as a warrior . . .
"a man of honor experienced in the battle and willing to lead
and take on the fight." Positive characteristics for a warrior
include competitiveness, achievement driven, leader, high
personal code, etc. These all leave us with very big shoes to
fill. I know firsthand from Saint Joan of Arc, Central Catholic, and Michigan State just how big those shoes were. But
just as there are strengths to being a warrior, there are also
weaknesses: ego-driven, hard on relationships, inflexible,
and self-destructiveness, to name a few. Carole has a saying
in her psychology practice that "life is all about learning."

With that thought in mind, Dick got a PhD in life . . .

His amazing talents translated into outward success as well as major setbacks. When I combine his experiences (both the highs and lows) with what we now recognize as literally decades of progressive suffering from CTE dementia . . . Dick's last twenty-plus years were very troubled. With the benefit of hindsight, it is easy for me and those around him to track the debilitating signs of the disease: withdrawal; aggression; depression; failing executive functioning leading to judgment, decision-making, and financial management issues; anxiety; panic attacks; paranoia; and even psychotic breaks, with the final result being an overall diminishment of mental and physical capacities. As a warrior, his natural instinct was to cover these up by fighting back . . . believing he could overcome . . . as a warrior does . . . as he had always done.

As the saying goes in sports, "The great ones play hurt." This was no more evident than at his induction at the Stark County High School Football Hall of Fame. I knew I would have to do his acceptance speech, which I was honored to do. But that wasn't enough for Dick, as he insisted on taking the mic to talk. For several minutes, he held the audience's attention, attempting to say what was important to him. He could not articulate a single audible word, as much as he tried. What everyone in the room did hear, however, was the heart of a champion.

Participating in Dick's life and reliving it over during the last few weeks was a fantastic journey that I'll treasure as a brother. Growing up with parents who showered us with love and solid direction, Dick's life started here at Saint Joan of Arc in grade school as an altar boy, voice in the choir, student, and athlete. That led to a phenomenal student-athlete experience at Central Catholic and to Michigan State University, where he graduated on time and received five varsity letters in baseball and football. Afterward, canoe trips with older brother John, vacations together, building a family, and spending time in Minnesota are just some of the remembrances that will be missed. As his career in business developed, many achievements followed, with his responsibilities at IBM, NML, and Mid-States Equipment.

For me, however, it's the loss of a brother who always bailed me out of difficulties while growing up. Dick gave me solid advice when I was about to make a wrong turn. He was helpful beyond expectation on projects involving time and labor. And his subtle yet powerful words of encouragement—just when I needed it—about how proud he was of me and how he always referred to me with others as "a winner" left their indelible mark. In football, the first rule of an offensive lineman is to protect your quarterback. I could have never asked for a better quarterback to protect.

I found a place to conclude this eulogy in Leo Tolstoy's *War and Peace*, which is probably appropriate considering the time I've taken. The quote comes from the character Prince Andrew: "Love is life itself. All, everything that I understand, I understand only because I love. Everything is, everything exists, only because I love. Everything is united by love alone. Love is God, and to die means that I, a particle of love, shall return to this eternal source called God."

The wound we feel now losing Dick—as a father, brother, uncle, friend, or teammate—will turn to a scar. We just have to remember that the scar we carry is a sign that the wound has healed and that life is moving forward.

ACKNOWLEDGMENTS

Each time I approach a writing project, my conviction is tested by the many pot holes in the road to completion. Invariably, those pot holes are filled with the help and support by people who ultimately influence the outcome. *Unintended Impact: One Athlete's Journey from Concussions in Amateur Football to CTE Dementia* was no exception.

In some respects, these challenges were far more difficult than those in previous fiction works. This story is a creative nonfiction work, sometimes seen as a memoir. I had to be accurate with my memories and had to tell the truth as I knew it. This was daunting, considering the story spanned over sixty-plus years. And throughout the journey, I certainly didn't want to throw my brother under the bus with incomplete knowledge or conclusions. It had to be honest, truthful, sensitive, and open. The list of supporters is long.

- My wife, Carole, lived most of this story with me. Combined with her knowledge of psychology and experience with patients affected with chronic brain disorders, she was helpful and a wonderfully supportive "go-to" partner, guiding me away from most of the pitfalls of my own preconceived judgments.

- Mike Proebstle and Patty Pae, Dick's children, lived the confusion and debilitation of their father's disorder with no road map. Being open with their experiences and emotions exposed the underbelly of the beast (CTE) and the harsh reality of their roles in searching for a solution. Mike and Patty are the hero and heroine, as they dealt with their own set of complex and undefined medical, behavioral, relationship, financial, and emotional challenges in attempting to define and solve the problems. Their tireless contributions to shape *Unintended Impact* were offered in an unbiased and forthright manner.

- The many interviewees who permitted me to poke and prod into their connections with Dick and who added context to the story include (alphabetically): Ken Bankey, Jim Bray, Diane Demont, Mike Fay, Terry Glarner, Tim Helline, Steve Juday, Charlie Migyanka, John Mullin, Paula Proebstle, Jimmy Raye, Bill Rearick, George Saimes, Jane (Matthews) Steiner, and John Walsh.

- Pat and Delores Gallinagh provided an early review of the unfinished manuscript that was very instrumental in shaping the direction and tone of the story.

- At Michigan State University, Paulette Martis in the Sports Information office helped with the research details behind Dick's football experience at MSU. And the medical records team at the Olin Health Center on campus willingly resurrected Dick's football injury records from the '60s.

ACKNOWLEDGMENTS

- The overwhelming support from the Sports Legacy Institute—including Dr. Robert A. Stern's foreword, Chris Nowinski's leadership, and Lisa McHale's family support—was professional, generous, and compassionate. The Sports Legacy Institute's continued worldwide leadership will influence the safety for all athletes in contact or collision sports.

- Online and in-print literature is abundant for serious research. Two books that were most helpful to me were:

  - Linda Carroll and David Rosner, *The Concussion Crisis: Anatomy of a Silent Epidemic,* Simon & Schuster (2012).

  - Chris Nowinski, *Head Games,* Drummond Publishing Group (2006, 2011).

- The cooperative and talented support received from the team at Beaver's Pond Press, my new publisher, was enthusiastic and professional. Special appreciation goes to Angela Wiechmann for editing my work for the first time. Her editing expertise and special knowledge of concussions and CTE were skillfully applied in successfully bringing this effort to conclusion, while respecting and complementing my writing style.

I would like to think that *Unintended Impact* will make a difference in how people view those with CTE dementia, how vulnerable they are, and how the sport of football is approached going forward. Portions of the book's proceeds will be shared with the Michigan State University Spartan Fund (Dick Proebstle Scholarship Fund AA204) and the Sports Legacy Institute. Information for both organizations can be found online. Your help is greatly appreciated.

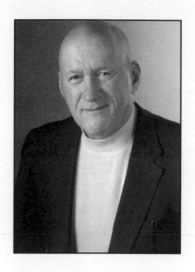

ABOUT THE AUTHOR

Jim Proebstle's first two novels have received outstanding reviews from readers and industry professionals. They have been recognized with many awards, including the Eric Hoffer Award, the Indie Book Award, and the International Book Award.

He and his wife, Carole, live in Deer Park, Illinois, and call northern Minnesota home for the summer months.

Proebstle received his BA and MBA from Michigan State University. He was fortunate enough to be a member of MSU's national championship football team in 1965 and earn academic honors. Jim and Carole are Spartans for life.